C000194240

Walking
The Isles of Islay, Jura and Colonsay

Clan Walk Guides

Walking
The Isles of Islay,
Jura and Colonsay

Walking Scotland Series
Volume 8

Mary Welsh
and
Christine Isherwood

First published Westmorland Gazette, 1996 as *Walks on Islay*
Revised edition published by Clan Books, 1999
New expanded edition published by Clan Books, 2005
Reprinted, with revisions, 2010

ISBN 978 1873597 25 5

Clan Books
Clandon House
The Cross, Doune
Perthshire
FK16 6BE

Printed and bound in Great Britain by
Bell & Bain Ltd., Glasgow

Authors' Preface

Islay, Jura and Colonsay are set in the sea like stepping stones between Scotland and Ireland. They are the southernmost islands of the Inner Hebrides. All three have miles of bleak moorland—and gardens where bamboo and palm trees flourish. Sheltered sea lochs and quiet sandy bays contrast with furious seas off rugged, cave-pitted cliffs. No part of the three is far from the sea, which is viewed on most of the walks in this book.

Each Island has its own distinctive characteristics. Islay is the most populated and is extensively farmed. Visitors must expect to find cattle and other farm animals on some of the routes described, and should be prepared to divert, or even abandon a walk if cattle seem to be threatening, especially during the calving season. It is particularly dangerous to attempt to take dogs across land occupied by cattle with calves.

Jura is largely wild, sparsely populated, with a trio of fine summits and just one single-track road. Colonsay, more remote of access, is an ideal location for birdwatchers and naturalists, with a benign climate, low rainfall and fine, sandy beaches. All these islands offer great walks, but many routes have no clear path and you will need your map, strong boots and good waterproofs.

In addition, the usual 'golden rules' for good, safe walking in wild countryside apply:

- On longer walks, take extra food and drink as emergency rations.

- Carry a whistle; remember six long blasts repeated at one minute intervals is the distress signal.

- Do not walk alone, and tell someone where you are going.

- If mist descends, return.

- Keep all dogs under strict control. Observe all 'No Dogs' notices—they are there for very good reasons.

Publisher's Note

Many of the walks described were originally published in *Walks on Islay* (first edition, 1996). All of these have been checked by the authors and the opportunity has been taken to extend several of them to offer ambitious walkers a more interesting challenge. Others have been approached from a different angle, or amended to take account of changes on the ground, and to improve the quality of the walk.

Several walks on Islay, and nearly all the Jura expeditions, are completely new. The Colonsay walks were first included in the volume *Walks on Tiree, Coll, Colonsay and a Taste of Mull* (1996), now superseded by vol. 10 in the Walking Scotland series: (*Walking the Isles of Mull, Iona, Coll and Tiree*) which does not take in Colonsay.

Readers who find anything incorrect or misleading in the walk descriptions are invited to inform us for future reference. The book sets out to be an entertaining and helpful guide, but neither authors nor publishers can be held responsible for any loss or injury that might be considered to result from its use.

FERRY ACCESS

There are daily sailings (at differing times) to either Port Ellen or Port Askaig on Islay from Kennacraig, Argyll. Argyll and Bute Council operate the Jura ferry from Port Askaig to Feolin; this runs daily, approximately once per hour. Ferries to Colonsay are infrequent.

At the time of going to press the Oban–Colonsay service runs:
In summer (B.S.T. period from late March to late October)
– OUT from Oban, Monday p.m. / BACK to Oban, Tuesday a.m. OUT and BACK same day on Thursday, Friday and Sunday (No Saturday service);
In winter months – OUT and BACK from Oban on Monday, Wednesday and Friday only.

There is now no ferry connection between Islay and Colonsay in the winter months. In summer, (end March to end October) on Wednesdays only, a vessel sails from Kennacraig via Port Askaig to Colonsay, and on to Oban, returning in the afternoon and evening by the same route. This is the only remaining direct public link between Colonsay and its Southern neighbours.

Contents

Contents continued page 7

Location Map

COLONSAY

Scalasaig

ORONSAY

JURA

The Paps

Port Askaig

Ballygrant

Bridgend

Bowmore

Bruichladdich

Port Charlotte

Portnahaven
Port Wemyss

ISLAY

Mull of Oa

Port Ellen

Loch Gruinart

Loch Indaal

Craighouse

N

10 Km

10 miles

Walking Scotland Series
from Clan Books

MARY WELSH has already compiled walkers' guides to each of the areas listed: material for guides covering the remaining parts of Scotland is being gathered for publication in future volumes.

Titles published so far:

1. WALKING THE ISLE OF ARRAN
2. WALKING THE ISLE OF SKYE
3. WALKING WESTER ROSS
4. WALKING PERTHSHIRE
5. WALKING THE WESTERN ISLES
6. WALKING ORKNEY
7. WALKING SHETLAND
8. WALKING THE ISLES OF ISLAY, JURA AND COLONSAY
9. WALKING GLENFINNAN: THE ROAD TO THE ISLES
10. WALKING THE ISLES OF MULL, IONA, COLL AND TIREE
11. WALKING DUMFRIES AND GALLOWAY
12. WALKING ARGYLL AND BUTE
13. WALKING DEESIDE, DONSIDE AND ANGUS
14. WALKING THE TROSSACHS, LOCH LOMONDSIDE AND THE CAMPSIE FELLS
15. WALKING GLENCOE, LOCHABER AND THE GREAT GLEN
16. WALKING STRATHSPEY, MORAY, BANFF AND BUCHAN
17. WALKING AROUND LOCH NESS, THE BLACK ISLE AND EASTER ROSS
18. WALKING CAITHNESS AND SUTHERLAND

Books in this series can be ordered through booksellers anywhere.
In the event of difficulty write to
Clan Books, The Cross, DOUNE, FK16 6BE, Scotland.

For more details, visit the Clan Books website at
www.walkingscotlandseries.co.uk

Islay

Machir Bay

1

Ballygrant to the Lily Loch

Park in Ballygrant, either on the side of the main road, beside the village shop or, opposite the village hall, grid ref 396662. To reach the latter, take the turn signposted Mulindry, opposite the shop. The car park is on the right.

Ballygrant is a small linear village. At its southern end stands a row of houses built for workers who obtained lead from the many mines on the slopes above the village. The village hall was once the old forge and the burn, over the wall on the right of the hall, once powered Ballygrant's Mill.

Lily Loch

Walk 1

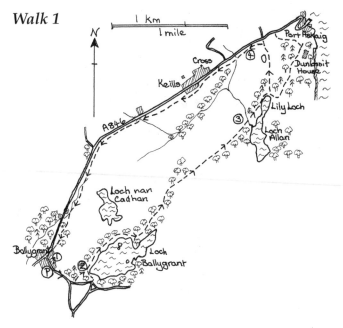

1. Take the turn, signposted Mulindry, opposite the shop and walk on to take the first estate road on the left. Continue up the road beside the walled woods to your left and then go on uphill to take the second entrance, on the left, into the deciduous woodland of Dunlossit Estate.

2. Stride the firm track to come beside Loch Ballygrant, with its crannog, a man-made island. Sit on the well placed seat to enjoy the loch and perhaps a pair of swans swimming serenely on the placid water. The loch is completely surrounded by trees, and is a riot of colour in autumn. Stroll on the pleasing way along the western shore of the loch to go past the track to Loch nan Cadhan.

3. Carry on along the main route to pass a track, going off right at the red bridge, which leads to the lovely Loch Allan, it too surrounded by conifers and rhododendrons. Eventually you reach the Lily Loch, its surface, at the right time of the year, almost covered with white water lilies. To the east side, banks of heather pleasingly slope down to the water's edge. Continue along the shore of the lovely pool and at a junction of tracks, take the one winding left and climbing gently through magnificent deciduous woodland. Follow it uphill and where it winds left to come close to the A846.

11

Waterlilies

4. At the time of writing this walk, much of this excellent track was completed, enabling walkers to return to Ballygrant, avoiding the sometimes busy road. The track is wide and easy to walk and makes exciting little diversions into the countryside. Three-quarters of a mile along, you might wish to join the road and visit the village of Keills to see its ruined medieval church and the shaft of an ancient cross. In the early nineteenth century, houses were built here for linen weavers from the mainland, to work on flax grown locally.

5. Return to the track and stroll on to Ballygrant.

Practicals

Type of walk: This is a glorious walk, particularly good when a gale makes walking the shores of the island rather heavy going.

Distance: 6 miles/9.5km
Time: 3 hours
Maps: OS Explorer 352, Landranger 60

Dunlossit—An Cladach

Park next to the village shop at Ballygrant on the A846, grid ref 396664, or by the village hall, grid ref 397663. To reach the latter take the turn, signposted Mulindry, opposite the shop.

Dun Bhoraraig, Islay's only iron-age broch stands, strategically, on a hillock (619ft/198m), above the Sound of Islay. It was once a galleried tower, 50ft/15m in height. It is believed to have been constructed between 100 BC and AD 100. Little remains today, but there are traces of a gallery, entrance and a circular outer wall. The dun may have been a rich man's house where local people went for protection in times of danger. From the dun there is a glorious view of the Paps of Jura and the Sound. To the north you can see the mountains of Mull. To the south, over Gigha and the Mull of Kintyre, the Arran mountains stretch along the skyline. To the west lies the west coast of Islay.

Paps of Jura from Dun Bhoraraig

13

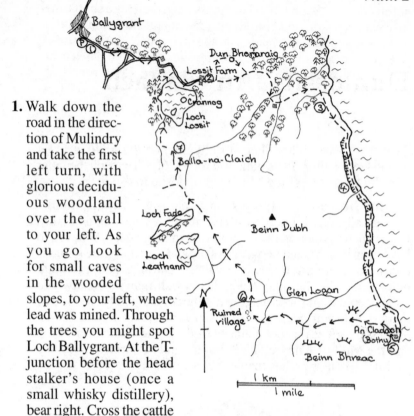

1. Walk down the road in the direction of Mulindry and take the first left turn, with glorious decidu-ous woodland over the wall to your left. As you go look for small caves in the wooded slopes, to your left, where lead was mined. Through the trees you might spot Loch Ballygrant. At the T-junction before the head stalker's house (once a small whisky distillery), bear right. Cross the cattle grid and continue up onto the open slopes with Loch Lossit away to the right. To the left are the remains of an old limekiln that might have been associated with seven houses that once stood on the crannog in the loch. A short distance along stands Lossit farm, the highest farm on Islay. Read the instructions on the next gate, which tell you that deer stalking takes place between July 1 and February 15 and gives you the phone number (01496 840232) to ask if it is in progress on the day you wish to walk.

2. Go through the gate and leave the track to climb up, left, to visit Dun Bhoraraig. After a pause on the top, descend the steepish slope to rejoin the track and stride on. In summer the way is lined with colourful flowers. Follow the track as it continues downhill, passing through beds of yellow iris and over a burn. Continue

14

towards a sturdy barn and pass to the right of it. Go on along the reinforced track. Soon it becomes grassy and then for a short time less clear. Press on ahead in the same general direction until a good track appears and leads you through a deer gate out onto open rough heather pasture above the shoreline. The gate is set in a wall that stretches for 25 miles across Islay to prevent deer from getting into the arable land.

3. Carry on along a narrow path that runs parallel with, but well above, the Baleachdrach shore. Pause often to enjoy the magnificent view across the Sound to Jura and along the northeast coast of Islay. Look for grey seals on the rocks and eider ducks on the water. Notice the rip tide as the currents meet in the Sound. Continue ahead on a narrow, and sometimes indistinct, path through heather until you come to a large bay lined with cliffs. Here move down close to the shore, from where you will see several caves and pleasing waterfalls tumbling over the cliffs. It is in one of these caves that Alexander Baldwin (Baldie), a local resident, made illegal whisky, with the nearby waterfall keeping it cool and the cave hiding it from the excise men. Eventually he was caught and transported to America.

4. Continue on under the cliffs choosing the easiest route. Sometimes you will need to clamber over rocky protrusions and care should be taken if the boulders are wet. Look out for peregrine, sparrowhawk, barn owl and golden eagle. Go on to pass a 'stranded' arch and walk on to step across Glen Logan Burn. If the burn is in spate you may have difficulty in crossing. Look for some timber, which other walkers have used as a bridge, to help you across. If you cannot cross, this will have to be the point of return. Beyond the burn, walk on along the winding shore to reach An Cladach, a Mountain Bothy Association hut that has been constructed from one of the ruins of the one-time tiny settlement here, possibly the house of old Baldie. This is a good place for lunch.

5. Then wind round the far side of the bothy and follow a path behind it that climbs steeply, slanting right as it climbs the east and then the north side of Beinn Bhreac. Cross a col which joins a spur to the main ridge. Carry on along the indistinct path as it weaves between two pools. Remain high on the slopes of Beinn Bhreac above Glen Logan, keeping above the bracken and using deer trods as you go. From here look to the skyline where you might

see the deer peering down on you. Look ahead to see a 'green island' with a ruin on it. Then descend the intervening glen before climbing to the ruin from where you can look down Glen Logan to the Sound. The ruins are the remains of shielings, huts, where women and children stayed in the summer looking after the cattle as they fed on the high-level plentiful, lush grass. There are more ruins on either side of the grassy patch, the greenness evidence of past cultivation.

6. Then set off on a clearer path to descend and step across the infant Glen Logan burn, before ascending once more across the open moorland, with Loch Leathann coming into view to your left. Press on keeping well above and, well right, of the loch again using indistinct paths. Carry on to pass the east end of Loch Fada where you join a track and pass through a gate. Soon leave the track to go right and climb to Balla-na-Claich (the Stony Township) to see signs of old lead workings.

7. Then begin your descent towards Loch Lossit. Join another track and go through a gate in the fence, first checking whether it is electrified. Stroll on along a track, which brings you to a gate into the lovely woodland beside the Lossit loch. Beyond, head on to pass the treatment works at its north end. Stride on the continuing reinforced track and, at the T-junction, turn left to walk your outward route.

Barn owl

Practicals

Type of walk: Challenging. An excellent walk for seasoned hill walkers who can read a map and use a compass. Walking boots and waterproofs essential.

Distance:	10 miles/16km
Time:	5–6 hours
Maps:	OS Explorer 352, Landranger 60

3

Ardtalla to Proaig

Park in the yard, to the left of Ardtalla, grid ref 466545. This lies at the end of the metalled road that continues on beyond the end of the A846 at Ardbeg.

Proaig, meaning 'broad bay' in Old Norse, was given its name by the Vikings who settled here, attracted by the green pastures, close to the River Proaig. The families of the Lords of the Isles, the chiefs of the MacDonalds, who ruled the Hebrides from the twelfth century to the fifteenth century, lived at Proaig farm. It was one of the most prosperous and important on Islay. After that time, descendants of the chiefs built successive houses here. It was occupied until the 1930s.

Children who lived at Proaig not only walked the track of this ramble but continued on for two miles to the school at Ardmore. The track was used by horse and carts 30 years ago and today four-wheel-drive vehicles take stalkers along it on their way into the hills. The views out to sea are delightful as you go.

Kildalton Cross

Kildalton cross stands in the graveyard of the ruined Kildalton Church. The weathered cross is carved, probably by a sculptor from Iona, from one piece of local grey-green epidorite. It is a ringed cross with its arms intact. Go inside the twelfth or thirteenth century church, the walls and gable ends of which are still standing. Look for the fine grave-slab with an effigy of a knight in armour.

1. Go through a gate from the parking area to follow the track into pasture and stroll on to pass through the next gate. Carry on over open ground, with only scrubby bushes edging the burns, to go through the next gate. Then, after less than half a mile, you come to a fence across the track. Look for the nearby stile to cross it and stride on over the rather bleak moorland.

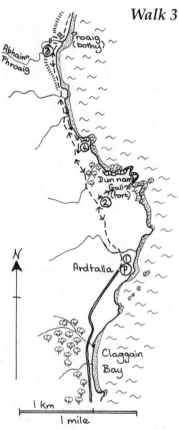

Walk 3

2. After about another mile and before you drop down towards a burn, leave the track, right, to reach a small promontory to see the scant remains of Dun nan Gall (the fort of strangers) which faces north east. Then return to the track and walk on. Soon it moves closer to the coastline, with superb views across the Sound of Islay to Jura. Stroll on, following the track as it begins to descend towards the valley of the River Proaig, with the old farm buildings beyond. As you go notice how the grass becomes lush and greener, evidence of a prosperous farm years ago. The track takes you along a raised beach, now stranded high and dry, the sea-level being higher at the end of the last ice-age.

3. Then you reach the side of the River Proaig, which you cross by a metal sleeper some distance upstream from the path, or, if the burn is not in spate, you might prefer to wade across lower

Fallow deer

down the burn towards the shore. Then walk across to the old farmhouse and the steadings, all derelict except for one that has been renovated as a bothy and a good place to have your picnic. After browsing around the old buildings, return across the river and head along the shore, walking over sand and shingle and clambering over rocks. Continue on for about a mile.

4. When you have crossed the Allt nam Bodach, as it crosses the shore after tumbling down the slopes, your will find your way blocked by a cliff face. Here begin your scramble up the shrub-lined gully onto the flat ground above. Head inland to pick up your outward route. Turn left and walk the track to Ardtalla. Then begin your return drive. After a mile or so you reach lovely Claggain Bay. This has a shingle and sandy beach, with superb views to Kintyre. Here you might like to pause and watch for otters and divers.

5. Then drive on and notice as you go the old Ardmore school, still with its bell tower and think of the children from Proaig who had this extra distance to cover after walking the track. Drive on for another 1½ miles to take a turn, on the left, signposted to Islay's great treasure, Kildalton church and cross, where you will want to linger. Here you may see fallow deer, no doubt escaped from someone's herd.

Red-throated diver in winter plumage

6. Before you leave this lovely part of Islay, drive on to the first house on the left at Lagavulin and park tidily. Then walk an unsignposted left turn that leads towards a short grassy track to the foot of Dunyveg castle. The crumbling, unstable, romantic ruin, with not much more than a corner of its keep still standing, dates from the seventeenth century, with traces of an earlier castle visible. It provided a safe, well hidden anchorage for the ships of the Lords of the Isles. Across the bay stands Lagavulin distillery, one of three to be found here. It produces single malt whisky.

Practicals

Type of walk: The track to Proaig takes you across pastures and over moorland on a fairly level way. It can be waterlogged in parts after heavy rain. There are several burns to cross and only one has a footbridge, so be prepared for a sometimes wet walk. The return is made along the shore, before a steepish climb up a rocky gully.

Distance: 6 miles/9.5km
Time: 3 hours
Maps: OS Explorer 352, Landranger 60

NB *Check with the estate gamekeeper (Tel 302218) during the stalking season before commencing this walk.*

4

Solam, the fever village

Parking isn't easy. Take coffee at the Ardbeg distillery and ask if you may park there, grid ref 415464. Or tuck into a space near the telephone box on the A846, where the road turns into the distillery.

The village of **Solam** was wiped out by cholera in about 1865–6. It is believed the plague had been brought by shipwrecked sailors taken in by the villagers. In order to contain the disease, nobody was allowed to leave the village. Food was brought in by friends and relatives from well beyond Solam and placed on a stone. One day the food remained, untouched, and then people bringing it knew that all the village had died. Eventually the houses were burnt down. Only a well, remains of wall bases, mounds and several stones remain.

Lazybeds were narrow strips raised by throwing soil on them from trenches dug along either side. The trenches served as drainage channels. Seaweed was added to the soil and then potatoes were grown in the beds.

Islay has seven **distilleries**, plus the maltings at Port Ellen, all of

Carved Face, Solam
(said to be Robert Burns)

which are sited where there are ample supplies of water and peat, both of which give the whiskies their distinctive flavour. There are three distilleries along the south coast beyond Port Ellen, Laphroaig, Lagavulin and Ardbeg. Ardbeg lies three miles along where the A-road ends. The continuing road is unclassified.

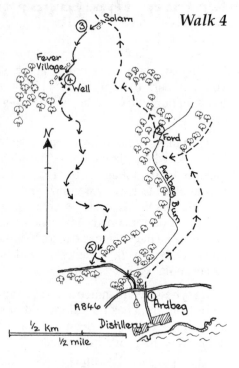

Walk 4

1. From the Ardbeg distillery walk back to the A846, cross and, slightly right, take the rising gated track bearing north-east. This leads out into open pasture, where you might spot fallow deer. Wind right to the next gate and, once through, curve left. After the next gate turn left and follow the track as it drifts right round the steep hillside, to your right, to come level with woodland. Then cross, left, over the grass to go through a gate into the trees. Beyond a track leads to the Ardbeg Burn, which you ford on rough stones. (This can be difficult if it is in spate.) Walk on through the trees on a grassy track.

2. Follow the track uphill and after emerging from the woodland go on up an indistinct curving way over moorland. Carry on across lazybeds to come beside a wall on your right, which runs up to the right of a steep heather-clad ridge. Continue up and once beyond the ridge, walk left to see the ruins of Solam farm. Just below the farm is a fine carving of a face on a rock.

3. Walk on along under the slopes of the ridge, now on your left. Wind round, left, of the end of the ridge to cross a small stream and then head, right, towards a very green grassy hillock. As you go look for a flat squarish stone, where it is thought the food was placed for the fever stricken folk.

22

4. Then cross, left, to the foot of another ridge to see the village well (visitors have thrown in pennies here) tucked into the foot of a cleft in the tall cliffs. Close by are more remains of houses. Just beyond the ridge, wind left up a small valley and then, with a good view of the small islands off Ardbeg and out to sea, head towards them. Go down a slope and then turn right to make a wide loop, on paths, and then left across some boggy ground. Join a good track and wind round, right, with another ridge on your right. Pass through shrubby woodland to a gate you can see ahead.

5. Go ahead and then over some brambly ground to descend, left, to a road. Turn left and walk on to cross a bridge over the Ardbeg Burn to return to where you have parked.

Meadow pipit

Practicals

Type of walk: An enjoyable walk back into the nineteenth century but one that can be wet underfoot. Walking boots or Wellingtons essential.

Distance: 3½ miles/5.5km
Time: 2–3 hours
Maps: OS Explorer 352, Landranger 60

5

Port Ellen

Park in the public car park at the north-west end of Port Ellen, grid ref 336456.

The houses of **Port Ellen** curve around its shapely bay, sheltered under the Oa. It is Islay's largest village, has its own maltings, and is also the main Caledonian MacBrayne ferry terminal for the island. Walter Frederick Campbell, the laird, started to build the village in the 1820s and named it after his first wife Eleanor.

The chapel, Cill Tobar Lasrah, is believed to be named after an Irish female saint called Lasair. The tiny ruin has two small slabs of stone standing at the entrance to the sanctuary. Each of the stones has a hole through it. Local belief is that they are marriage stones and that the wedding couple joined hands through one of the holes. South of Kilbride farm are the scant remains of Kilbride Chapel, dedicated to St Brigid, another Irish saint.

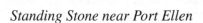

Standing Stone near Port Ellen

24

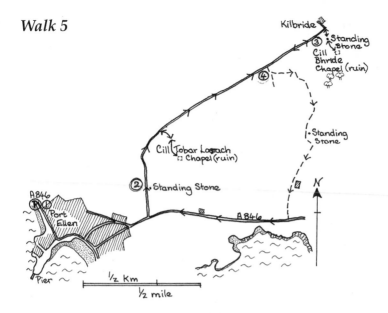

1. Wander along the attractive seafront and through the pleasing village and then set off along the A846 in the direction of Ardbeg. Ignore a left turn that leads back into Port Ellen and then take the next left turn, a minor road to Kilbride farm. Walk up the gently ascending way for 150m. Opposite a farm gate, climb the easy-to-miss stile over the wall on your right. Head across the pasture to view the magnificent standing stone, heavily encrusted with lichen. Then return to the road.

2. Walk on up the narrow road and follow it as it bears steadily right, to come to the fourth farm gate on the right, since you left the A-road. Beyond, strike ahead over the pasture, keeping to the left of a low mound. Carry on aiming for the left of the next and larger mound. Just over the low brow lie the ruins of the little chapel with the 'marriage stones'. Return to the gate and turn right to continue up the road. Ignore the track that turns off right and carry on ahead towards the farm.

3. Where the road bears left towards the farm buildings, pass through a gate on the right and walk to another splendid standing stone. Stroll on to climb a hillock and look down towards a small wood. Just before it you can see the outline of a small building, the remains of Kilbride Chapel, which you may wish to visit.

25

4. Return to the farm road, turn left and walk on to take the hedged track on the left, which you ignored previously. This descends pleasingly, through moorland at first, towards the main road. As you go look for yet another standing stone on the left. Beyond, lies the blue water of a reservoir where you might spot tufted duck and wigeon. At the main road, turn right. Walk on to return towards Port Ellen, noticing the fine walls which edge the road, constructed with their stones placed vertically, rather than horizontally, as is more usual.

Pair of twites

Practicals

Type of walk: A quiet, easy walk through peaceful countryside to view three huge standing stones and two ruined chapels.

Distance:	4 miles/6.5km
Time:	2–3 hours
Map:	OS Explorer 352, Landranger 60

Carraig Fhada lighthouse and the Singing Sands

Use the car park, grid ref 344456, off the minor road to the Oa. To reach this, leave Port Ellen by the road that runs left of the Maltings, signposted The Oa. Ignore the right turns to Bowmore and Kintra and then, in less than a quarter of a mile turn left just after a cemetery on the left and park in the car park.

Carraig Fhada Lighthouse stands on offshore rocks, connected to the mainland by a bridge and concrete causeway. It is unusual in being an early example of the use of solar power, and was erected by the laird Walter Frederick Campbell in memory of his wife, Lady Eleanor, after her death in 1832. He also named Port Ellen, the village and harbour which he founded, after her.

Carraig Fhada lighthouse

Along the lovely stretch of white sand, **Traigh Bhan**, are scattered strange tortured, heavily eroded outcrops. The name 'singing sands' is given to the sands because of the sound the wind makes as it blows over the grains.

Walk 6

1. From the car park, go gently downhill towards the shore, by a small group of new houses. Follow the metalled road to the right up the hill, with banks of heather on either side. As you ascend look left to see the lighthouse down below. Where the road swings right take the left fork, and leave this track leftwards by one of several grassy paths that descend easily over a sloping pasture, the driest following heather at the edge of the pasture. These paths all take you downhill to pass between the shallow dunes on to the beach. Here you will want to linger.

2. When you have made the sands sing by scuffing your heels and have watched the birds over the waves and along the shoreline, turn left to walk to the high jagged rocks at the end of the strand. Here veer a little left to take a short grassy path to a gate. Beyond climb the steps to a higher level where you have a fine view of the jagged coastline and perhaps see the feral goats that feed on the seaweed. Go on to take more steps up the slope to a signpost that directs you left. Pass through gates on a path that takes you around and above the back of the house on the shore.

3. Descend to walk, left, along the shoreline track and look for otters, eiders, and more feral goats. As you go it is hard to imagine that the sea once came up to the foot of the cliffs on your left. On reaching the old cemetery, go through the gates to see the ruins of the thirteenth century chapel. Look inside to see a carving of a knight. Then return to the gate and turn left to walk along a sandy path through more shallow dunes. Take your choice of paths to continue through the now much taller dunes to come to the side of the Cornabus Burn, hurrying out to sea. Look across the river to see a fine but roofless bathing hut. This was built for John Ramsey's family who walked from their house, Cairnmore, through the woodlands to bathe. It is set into the cliff, with heather-covered crags on either side and woodland above.

28

4. Climb the dunes behind, rising above the river, and return towards the modern cemetery. Go through a gate to rejoin the track 50 yards before the car park.

Wild goats

Practicals

Type of walk: Short but quite delightful.

Distance: 3 miles/5km
Time: 2 hours
Maps: OS Explorer 352, Landranger 60

7

The Mull of Oa

Park in a small parking area at the gate to the access track to Upper Killeyan farm, grid ref 282423. To reach this take the left turn, signposted Mull of Oa (pronounced O), to the left of the Maltings at Port Ellen. Follow more signposts for five miles, up a narrow road with passing places.

A pleasing walk (about 1 mile) takes you over rising pastures to a **massive monument** on the edge of very high cliffs. It commemorates 650 American sailors and soldiers, who died in two naval disasters in the closing months of the 1914–18 war. Many of the bodies were washed up at the foot of the cliffs.

Mull of Oa

Walk 7

1. Pass through the gate beyond the parking area and follow the well waymarked route. Stiles and gates take you through the fences and duckboards carry you over wet areas as you near the top of the magnificent cliffs. The huge monument seems to draw you on. Its sad legend seems even more poignant set on this austere, lonely outpost of Islay. From this high point, on a clear day, you can see the coast of Ireland. Enjoy, with care, the superb view of the coastline. Look for choughs circling over the cliffs and perhaps a golden eagle spiralling upwards.

2. Then drop down from the monument, north-west, to a fence. Continue outside the fence, or inside if you are nervous of heights. Carry on to cross the narrow burn, the Sruthan Ruadh, and go on along the cliff edge, walking with care and stopping to enjoy the spectacular views. Here rock doves fly off from the cliff face as you pass. Cross another small stream, then move away from the edge to climb a stile in the fence directly ahead. Remain well away from the cliffs now and begin to drift slightly right, to cross two more streams. Head on in the same general direction to come to the edge of a deepish gully, An Gleann. Here goats often graze.

31

Choose a good place to cross the burn after dropping down the banking. Once over turn right and climb the far side of the gully. At the top strike over the pasture towards the houses at Lower Killeyan, soon to join a track and then a road.

3. Turn right and walk the minor road as it passes through extensive moorland until you can take the right turn back to the parking area.

Rock doves

Practicals

Type of walk: The waymarked route to the monument is distinct and a steady, delightful climb all the way. The return route is over rough pasture until you reach Lower Killeyan. Choose a good day so that you can really enjoy this challenging walk with such dramatic views. During the breeding season, dogs may be prohibited, to protect ground-nesting birds: please obey signs at the car park.

Distance: 4 miles/6.5km
Time: 2–3 hours
Maps: OS Explorer 352, Landranger 60

8

Kintra

Park in the signed parking area at Kintra Farm, grid ref 321483. To reach this keep left at Port Ellen Maltings and follow the signposted Oa road, then following the Kintra road sign for two-and-a-half miles.

This is a grand walk. It has all the best that Islay has to offer: a standing stone, three deserted townships, an ancient chapel, a cup-marked rock, a magnificent sea stack, a natural arch, a deep spectacular chasm, two waterfalls, otters, seals, eagles, choughs, wild goats, natural woodland and sandy bays.

Choughs nest in cracks or fissures, in the roof or sides of a tidal cave, or in a hollow in a steep crag or cliff face. They also nest in ruined buildings, whose roof spaces imitate a cliff cave. Their bulky nests are made of roots or stems of heather, gorse or other plants, and lined with wool or hair. They probe short turf or excavate old cow pats for grubs. On this walk sit by the Soldier's Rock, a huge stack,

Soldier's Rock

33

and watch for the glossy black birds, cousins to raven, crows and rooks, as they glide gracefully, just below you, with their down-curved bills and legs a brilliant red. As they fly up you may hear them utter their distinctive call.

Walk 8

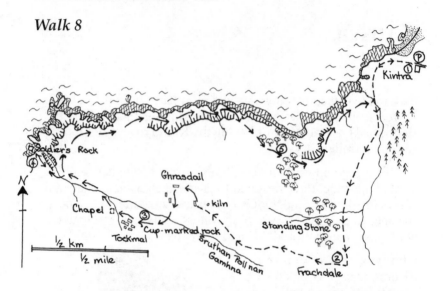

1. Follow the track to the left that winds above the shore. Look right to see the glorious 4-mile strand edging Laggan Bay. Ahead across the mouth of Loch Indaal, you can see the lighthouse on Orsay, off Portnahaven. Pass through the gate, on which a notice says, 'No dogs beyond this point'. Follow the good track, a former drove road, as it fords a stream and moves steadily out into moorland, where bog myrtle, rush, heather, bog asphodel, grass of Parnassus, marsh St John's wort, yellow mountain saxifrage and scabious flower during the summer months. As you climb steadily, notice lots of birch and willow which thrive in the native woodland to your right and, away to the left, the hill slopes are planted with conifers. Then birch, willow and huge banks of heather crowd the right side of the track which leads you towards the ruined crofthouse of Frachdale, high on the moorland.

2. Just before the ruin, follow the rising track, right. As you approach the gate in the fence, look right to see a tall standing stone. Pass through the gate and keep to the indistinct green path as it moves ahead through heather moorland. Aim for the ruined township

Choughs

of Ghrasdail. Look for the kiln, set into the slope on your right, before you reach the roofless dwellings. Then descend steadily left, passing remnants of old walls, to cross the narrow burn, Sruthan Poll nan Gamhna, just below the scrub.

3. Just before Tockmal, another ruined township of several crofthouses, look for a boulder with several small carved depressions, rings and spirals. Such boulders are known as cup-marked rocks. Some archaeologists believe these markings might have been used as a prehistoric system of waymarking. Continue to a narrow tributary of the main burn, on your left. Step across at a suitable place to look for traces of the sanctuary chapel and graveyard. In summer this is almost completely hidden by bracken. Cross back over the tributary and main burn, to avoid some very wet walking, and go on towards the shore. Just before it enters a deepening gully, cross back again. From here care should be taken, especially if children are walking. The burn at first tumbles in small falls and then, as the gully becomes immensely deep, it drops elegantly over stepped rocks to plummet far below. Proceed along the gully edge to cross over a natural rock arch in the cliff. From here there is a spectacular view of Soldier's Rock, a fine stack with glistening veins of quartz. Below where the cliffs drops sheer to the water, is a deep pool, Slochd Maol Doirdh. You will want to have a long pause here.

4. From here, the terrain becomes more challenging, with walkers left to choose their own route through heather moor and difficult birch scrub; you may prefer to retrace your steps and enjoy previous delights afresh. To continue, head east on sheep trods across flat ground above the main sea cliffs but below the higher line of cliffs

on the right, giving superb views seawards. After about a km the path rises to skirt a deep gully, where care is required, before heading down to the corner of a fence where there is a fallen gate.

5. Just before you reach the quartzite cliffs at Port Alsaig, you will need to find a way through natural birch woodland.Slant up the hillside from the fence corner to reach a flatter grassy tongue rising along the top of the birch scrub. At the end of the green area continue gently uphill to pick up a faint trod running along the fellside to an open shoulder, where it becomes more defined. Follow this path through scrub and down an open slope then through birch woodland to emerge above a small walled reservoir. Continue round two sandy bays, overlooked by conical-shaped grassy peaks, to reach a good farm track. Soon after joining it, head left to the cliff edge again and walk on to see a pretty waterfall on the Abhainn Ghlas. Rejoin the farm track and cross the burn by one of the two fords (the upstream one is slightly shallower) to join your outward track. Turn left to return to the parking area.

Bog myrtle

Practicals

Type of walk: Challenging. Full of interest, with spectacular sea views.

Distance:	5 miles/8km
Time:	3 hours
Maps:	OS Explorer 352, Landranger 60

9

Fun walk
around Islay's airport

Park at Glenegedale, slightly north and on the other side of the A846
to the terminal building of Islay's airport, grid ref 332515.

The Big Strand bordering on Loch Indaal is the longest stretch
of sand on Islay. It runs from Laggan Point through Machrie to
Kintra. The Machrie golf links (south of this walk) were constructed
in 1892 by William Campbell and apart from a few changes made
in the 1980s the course remains very much the same as when it
was first constructed. The sand dunes provide natural hazards that
challenge most golfers.

Laggan Bay(Traigh Mhor)

1. Cross the road from the parking area and walk south for 100m, in
   the direction of Port Ellen. Take a pleasant track leading off right
   and follow it as it heads towards the ford over the Machrie River.
   Soon, and before it comes to the ford, the way brings you close to
   the side of the river, where a raised pebble area in its bed generally
   makes it easy to cross. The track continues on the ford, where you
   might prefer to cross. After a long spell of rain both may be too

37

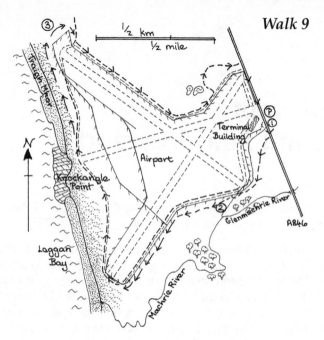

difficult to cross and it would be better to start the walk from the other side of the airport, returning from the shore by the same route, unless you are happy to paddle.

2. Once you have crossed the river stroll on, following the track left. Then continue as it winds right, along an old runway, above sand dunes, with the blue waters of Laggan Bay stretching away into the distance. Halfway along this section is Knockangle Point, the supposed site of the first inn on Islay. Carry on along the asphalted surface. Towards the end of this section, you can gain easy access to the lovely stretch of golden sand without walking through the sand dunes. Here you might see eiders, common gulls, redshank, curlew, great northern divers and black-throated divers, depending on the time of year.

Great northern diver in winter

Redshank

3. Once past gate five of the airport, bear right and follow another old runway and continue on to the road (this would be your access route if you are unable to cross the Machrie River). Along this part of the walk those interested in aircraft will enjoy watching the small planes arrive and depart. On joining the road, turn right to walk back to the parking area.

Practicals

Type of walk: A fun walk with something for all the family.

Distance: 4 miles/6.5km
Time: 2 hours plus time spent on the sands
Maps: OS Explorer 352, Landranger 60

10

Bowmore

Park along Bowmore's Main Street, which leads up to Kilarrow parish church, grid ref 312597.

Bowmore is Islay's attractive capital. It has wide spacious streets and a pleasant square with several bench seats. From the square, at the bottom of the Main Street, look up to the splendid round Kilarrow parish church, with its octagonal tower and stone cupola, built by Daniel Campbell in 1767. Legend says that its shape allows for no corners for the devil to hide. The village of Kilarrow once stood near the shore at Bridgend, but the eighteenth

The Round Church,
Bowmore

century laird who built Islay house, felt that the village spoilt his view and he had it removed to Bowmore.

The **Burma Road** was constructed by men who had returned from the 1939–45 war. They named it after the railway built by prisoners of war in Burma. A comment from some of those working on the Islay road was that it seemed 'not much easier'.

The **Gartbreak cottages** were used by fishermen when there was not enough time to unload their catch and return to their homes before setting off for another spell at sea. Sometimes they had to spend several days in the simple cottages while a storm raged. At such time they could neither get home or go back to sea.

Walk 10

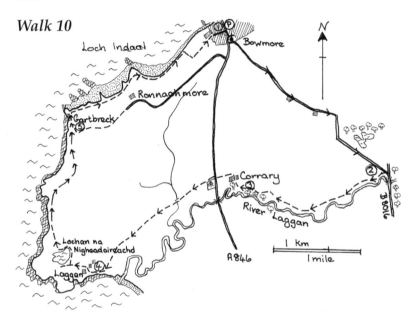

1. From the parking area walk uphill towards the delightful church, which you may wish to visit. Then after you leave the church wind left and, in a few step, take the narrow road that goes off left, south-east, in the direction of Cruach. The road, virtually traffic-free, passes through pastures, rising steadily for two and a quarter miles, until it comes very close to joining the B8016 (High Road) at Laggan Bridge.

2. Just before the junction take the track, going off right, known as the Burma Road. Stride the track for two miles as it passes through heather moorland, with the delightfully winding River Laggan idling through the valley to your left. Beyond the river stand several conifer plantations. Enjoy the gorse bushes, which are often in flower, where they sometimes enclose the path, the river banks and the nearby slopes.

3. Follow the track as it moves away from the river and passes to the right of Corrary farm. Soon after the farm buildings the track turns sharp left and goes on to join the A846. Cross and walk right for a few steps and then turn left onto another track. To your left lies a pleasing conifer plantation, with grassy glades, just the place for a picnic if the day is windy. Continue on along the track as it moves out into extensive moorland with the River Laggan out of sight, to your left, for much of the time as it hurries through its tree-lined banks. The track bears right when it reaches the coast. Pass two small bays, where tortured Torridonian rocks spike upwards. Here the tide comes racing in, crashing against the rocks, foaming white. Out to sea you can glimpse the hills of Ireland.

4. Carry on along the track as it winds right towards the out buildings and the fine house of Laggan. Beyond them turn left in the direction of Lochan na Nigheadaireachd. Just before the lochan, take another track which swings right and keeps close to its shore, on your left. Then follow the track as it leaves the shallow, partly reed-covered sheet of water, right, and head on keeping parallel with the sea inlet, Loch Indaal. Walk on along the track or move over to the green sward and walk just above the shoreline where

Scaup

C. M. Isherwood

42

you might spot oyster catchers, wigeon, bar-tailed godwits, golden plover, lapwing, redshank and curlews probing the sand. Continue on until you reach a gate to the right of Gartbreak. Stride on to a T-junction of tracks and turn left.

5. Pass the now derelict cottages that once provided temporary shelter for fishermen. Beyond is the renovated Gartbreak farm. Go through a small self-closing gate on to the turf above the shore and walk right. This is signed 'shore path' on fine slabs of stone. It leads you along the superb coastline, with views across Loch Indaal and ahead of Bowmore. Ignore the footpath to Ronnachmore and carry on along the shore to the next signed path. Step across a small ford and turn left. Beyond, a track continues onwards and brings you to the side of Bowmore's secondary school. Head on down the road until you reach the centre of the town. Here you might find time, before you return to your car, to walk, left, to the jetty. Offshore, depending on the time of year, you might see common scoters, grebes, eiders, mergansers, scaup, whooper swans and divers.

Barnacle Geese

Practicals

Type of walk: A pleasing mainly level walk, passing through quiet pastures, moorland, and along a lovely stretch of Loch Indaal.

Distance: 11 miles/17km
Time: 5–6 hours
Maps: OS Explorer 352, Landranger 60

11

Dun Nosebridge

Park in a lay-by, grid ref 364598, on the north side of the road, on the north side of Mulindry Bridge. From Bridgend, take the narrow road, signposted Mulindry and drive for two miles. Pass Neriby House and a cottage. Drop down a slope to reach the lay-by.

John McCorquodale, born in 1829, describes Dun Nosebridge, in his journal, as 'An **old Danish fort** surrounded by three semicircular mounds or ramparts, rising one above the other, all covered in beautiful green grass in winter and summer, the prettiest hill that can be seen anywhere.'

It is suggested that the hill-fort was occupied by late Bronze Age and early Iron-age people, who would have lived inside in circular huts. The ramparts and ditches would then have been higher and deeper, the entrance closed by large wooden gates. The quaint name of the dun encourages you to seek it out. It is believed to be a corruption of a Norse word that means fort on a crag—an apt description.

Dun Nosebridge

1. Go through the gate on the left, immediately before the bridge. Walk the track, which is shadowed by hazels, with a tiny tributary

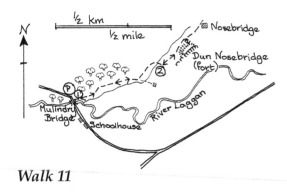

Walk 11

of the Laggan Burn to your right. Follow the main track through a gate and continue into oak and birch woodland, the haunt of chaffinches, siskins, coal, blue and long-tailed tits. As you emerge from the trees into an open area, look left to see more oak woodland stretching up the slope.

2. Ahead, on a prominent, long, raised crag, stands the fort. At the division of the track, take the lower right branch (unless flooded, when the left branch offers a higher but muddy alternative) and go on to the fort. Continue past the fort and turn right to take an easy way to ascend the ramparts and ditches. Take care as you

Great tit

approach the steep cliffs on the south-east side, which fall sheer to the flat land below. What a view from the top and what a defensive position. Beyond, hills lie to the west and higher hills to the east. Over a hump to the south you can see the sea.

3. On your return to Bridgend, you might like to park in the lay-by in front of the church on the right, just before the village. Cross the road and pass through a gate to visit the John Francis Campbell monument on the hill. He was the son of Walter Frederick Campbell and was a scholar, linguist, scientist and traveller. Stand at the foot of the obelisk for an extensive view of Loch Indaal and of the countryside around.

Siskin

Practicals.

Type of walk: The stroll to the hill-fort, Dun Nosebridge, is a delight.

Distance: 1½ miles/2.5km
Time: 1 hour
Maps: OS Explorer 352, Landranger 60

12

Bridgend and the River Sorn

Park beside the auction mart, on the A847, just before it joins the A846 at Bridgend, grid ref 334625. Or in the car park by the shop if there is a cattle or sheep sale.

The **woollen mill** was once an old waulkmill, a building where women sat round a large table pounding the linen, woven from flax grown close by. The mill stands beside the River Sorn, which here descends in a tempestuous waterfall, seen at its best from the road bridge. The mill was built in the late nineteenth century and on a guided tour you will be shown a rare spinning jenny and slubbing billy. Today the mill weaves tweeds and tartans for both export and the film industry. It

Woollen Mill and River Sorn

47

also weaves the material worn by the gamekeepers on the island and other estate workers, where needed. (For times of opening tel 01496 810563.)

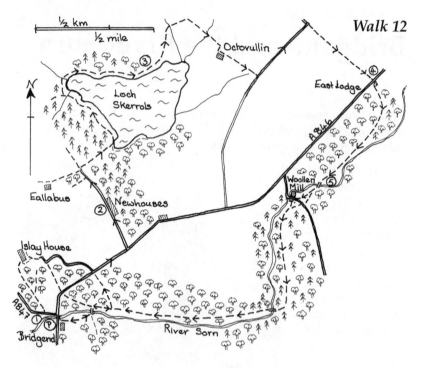

Walk 12

1. Walk right along the A847 for a short distance to join the A846. Turn right to reach the shops and petrol pumps with the hotel opposite. Cross the road, with care, and pass between two splendid gateposts to continue along a track. Take the first left turn and follow the delightful way, through woodland, on a gently descending way to cross the footbridge over the River Sorn. Walk ahead on a grassy swathe to join a track and turn right. Continue until you can take an acute left turn. Carry on along this through woodland to go through a gate to the A846. Walk right, facing the oncoming traffic, for ¼km, to take the first left turn, unsigned, on the other side of the road.

2. Pass two cottages on the right and then one on the left. Pass the gate to Eallabus beyond. Stroll on until you come to a cross of tracks,

where you turn right to walk through more glorious woodland until you reach Loch Skerrols (a few steps right gives you a pleasing view of the lovely stretch of water). Return to the track and carry on along the west side of the loch. Follow the track as it curves right, still through trees, to come to the outflow, Carabus Burn, which you ford. Continue on a rising track along the north side of the loch, passing under Scots pine and many sycamores.

3. Go through a gate and follow a well made track out on to open moorland, with fine views over rolling arable land and through glorious clumps of gorse. After a steady climb the track descends to cross an inflow to the loch. If after heavy rain this is too deep to wade, or too wide to jump, cross the burn on the 'waterwrack' or the 'sheep catcher', then climb the track beyond. Go on climbing gently towards Octovullin. Turn right to walk a short walled track and then on to pass the left side of the Dower House. Continue ahead to a narrow road. Here turn left and walk on to where the road makes a sharp left turn. Here walk, right, to descend another reinforced track to the A-road once more.

Snowdrops and primroses, Bridgend

4. Walk right for a few steps. Cross the road to stride the track that passes in front of East Lodge and stroll ahead on a glorious track through rampant deciduous woodland. Here in spring, first, snowdrops carpet the floor, followed by daffodils and primroses, and then bluebells, all before the leaves of the trees reduce the light. Here in this woodland many species of trees were planted but in the end only the salt-resistant sycamores survived. To your left is the Sorn River.

Wild daffodils

5. Cross a bridge over the river and then climb a little to take a track, right, that descends to a road. Turn right if you wish to visit the woollen mill. After your visit return up the road to take, almost at once, a new track uphill to join the main track, where you walk right. Continue on the lovely way still through the woodland. At the T-junction bear right and cross the bridge over the Sorn. At the next Y-junction go left until you see the grassy swathe, now left and taken earlier, to the footbridge over the Sorn once more. Bear right to walk to the road, through the gateposts to Bridgend.

Practicals

Type of walk: A good walk through extensive deciduous woodland and close to a lovely river and a delightful loch, with an optional visit to a woollen mill.

Distance: 5½ miles/9km
Time: 2–3 hours
Maps: OS Explorer 353, Landranger 60

13

Port Charlotte

Park tidily in the village, grid ref 254586

Port Charlotte, a pretty white-washed village, has a tiny harbour and an extensive view across Loch Indaal to Bowmore and down to the Oa peninsula. It began to be built in 1828 and was named after Walter Frederick Campbell's mother. The village had its own distillery but this was closed in 1929. Today the former warehouse is the site of the excellent Islay Field Centre, youth hostel and natural history research centre. Opposite, in a converted church, is the equally excellent Museum of Islay Life, founded in 1977.

Port Charlotte

1. Beyond (south of) the field centre, turn left and walk towards the shore. Bear left to cross the burn. If this is in spate and too difficult to cross, return to the road and walk right until you can get down to the shore. Once over the burn, stroll left along the sands and over rocky outcrops, continuing over two stiles, to reach the wall

Walk 13

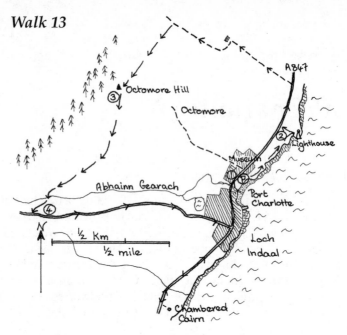

of the lighthouse, which stands on a dolerite dyke. Pause here and listen for the seals 'singing' and watch for gannets and shags diving for fish. You might also see an otter.

2. Turn left and head on to a gate, past loosestrife and meadow sweet at the right time of the year. Go on along the road, with glorious views across the sea loch. Once past a house named Tigh-na-Greine, turn left to walk a good track, which in early autumn is lined with blackberries. Where the track divides, take the left branch to pass a new house on your right. Beyond the wall gap, walk on until you can glimpse the tops of the sitka spruce in the plantation high up on the hillside. Look left to see, over the pasture, a gate at the junction of a wall and a fence and then choose the driest way to it. Beyond the gate and stile, climb steadily to Octomore Hill, from where you can often glimpse the Irish coast. Here you have a choice. You may prefer to descend a clear track to pass to the left of Octomore farm, and then go on downhill to return to Port Charlotte.

3. Alternatively, continue the walk from Octomore hill, by striding on over rough ground, keeping to the left of a grassy mound. Ahead, where a fence and a wall meet, go over the fence, on your left, by a stile. Descend steadily to the boundary fence, where you bear

left to pass through a gate. Head on downhill towards a telegraph pole and then on down again to cross the Abhainn Gearach. Climb diagonally right to a gate to the road.

4. Turn left and saunter along the narrow road towards Port Charlotte. Turn right at the main road and continue past the last house. Go through the gate on the left to walk across the end of the football pitch. Here stands a chambered cairn, a Neolithic burial site, divided into two chambers. Return towards Port Charlotte and turn right to walk along the edge of the bay to see the small pier. Continue through the village to where you have parked.

Purple loosestrife

Practicals

Type of walk: A pleasing walk over the pastures above Port Charlotte, from where there are excellent views. Strong shoes or boots required.

Distance: 4½ miles/7.4km
Time: 2 hours walking time
Maps: OS Explorer 353, Landranger 60

14

Gearach

Standing stone

Park on a grassy verge, on the north side of the road, grid ref 223594, just beyond the access track to Gearach farm. To reach this leave Port Charlotte by the narrow road, signposted Kilchiaran. Continue for two miles.

This tough three-and-a-half mile trek is a delightful challenge. After passing a twentieth century dam, which holds the water of Loch Gearach, the walk takes you back in time to various

Walk 14

periods of the island's history. You visit a nineteenth century ruined village, then a Bronze Age standing stone, before finally travelling forward in time again to climb a third or fourth century dun.

1. Walk back along the road to take a track on your left, leading towards Loch Gearach. Follow the way as it swings right and cross the Abhainn Gearach on boulders. Climb steadily to pass through a gate. At a junction of narrow paths, take the branch leading off right. Continue along this as it climbs a small hill and then descends to cross a wet area, where a little bog-hopping is required. Go on along the distinct path and follow it as it continues north, with Loch Gearach below to the left. The path leads deep into the quiet, lonely heather moorland. Keep to the right of a stone enclosure and press on.

2. The path is now indistinct. Aim for the first of the ruined houses of the village of Grimsay. Wander around the old buildings, taking care as you cross the rough tussocky pasture. Here you might spot a pair of eagles circling slowly overhead, steadily and effortlessly rising higher until they are lost from sight. From the village, look left (west) to see a standing stone. Then make your way towards it, choosing the easiest way and stepping across a narrow feeder stream on its way to the loch. Stand by the ten-foot high lichen-clad stone to obtain a good overall view of Grimsay. Then look south

Golden eagle

(the direction of the loch) to see a small conical hill, Dun Glas an Loin Ghuirm. Walk on to visit it.

3. While standing on the excellent vantage point, where sea pinks, tormentil and scabious flower in summer, look right (west) to see the corner of fencing edging a plantation of spruce. This is the way to continue. Walk towards the corner, choosing the driest way and negotiating a small stream. Go left (west) to another fence and follow it right, staying with it as it turns left and steadily descends to a good track. Turn right and follow the way to the road, where you have parked.

Lapwing

Practicals

Type of walk: An exhilarating, and often wet walk, up onto the moors of the Rhinns

Distance: 4 miles/6.5km
Time: 2–3 hours
Maps: OS Explorer 353, Landranger 60

NB No dogs allowed

15

The Rhinns and Ben Cladville

Park on one of several wide grass verges on the west side of Octofad farm, grid ref 217544, taking care not to block access for farm vehicles. The farm stands on the A847 and lies approximately half way between Portnahaven and Port Charlotte. Walk a few steps, north-east to the start of the track.

In the new edition of this volume published in 2005, we described what was believed to be a pleasant approach to the beautiful Lossit Bay, from the minor road less than a mile inland. Sadly, the experience of some walkers has not been pleasant, and we can no longer recommend this access. The fields and shoreline here are for much of the year grazed by a large herd of cattle, including a free-roaming bull and cows who are strongly protective of young calves.

In this edition, we suggest making for the vantage point of Ben Cladville instead, from which not only Lossit Bay but much

Lossit Bay

of the dramatic coastline northwards from Portnahaven can be seen. As there may also be livestock in this area, you should not take a dog with you.

Much of the **Rhinns** is high flattish moorland where peat is cut. The area is now managed by the farmers and landowners in conjunction with Scottish Natural Heritage. Large areas of the land has been planted with sitka spruce. From the Atlantic comes a sharp tangy breeze. Gaelic is spoken in nearby Port Charlotte and on the promontory.

Walk 15

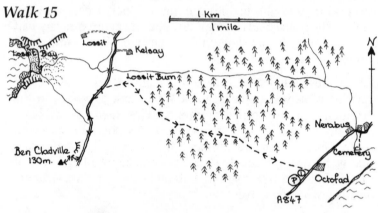

Merlin

Before or after your main walk, you might like to visit the signposted ancient **burial ground at Nerabus** on the south-east side of the A-road, where there is a small lay-by suitable for one car to park. It lies to the north-east side of Octofad farm. Walk down the track from the lay-by to wind round, right, beyond the wall of the modern burial ground, following the arrows for the Clan Donald burial ground. Go through a metal kissing gate, cross a small pasture and then on through another gate. Wander round the site, a wonderful green oasis among the rough pastures to see the low walls of a chapel, overgrown with vegetation. Look for the three grave-slabs, alas exposed to the elements.

1. From the parking area near Octofad farm, take the track that heads west across the Rhinns. As you go enjoy the ever-changing views of Islay and of Kintyre, Arran and sometimes of Ireland. The track is edged by a ditch colourful with wild flowers. Fortunately the conifers have been planted well back from the track and a wide swathe of heather thrives on either side. As you go you might see a hen harrier hunting along the edge of the ride.

2. At the end of the track, turn left along the road and follow it south for just under a kilometre to the foot of a distinctive small hill on the right, Ben Cladville. Pass underneath some low crags then slant to the right off the road and up the grassy slope to reach the summit trig, point. From here there are splendid views toward the beautiful village of Portnahaven and Frenchman's Rocks, and over Lossit Bay to the cliffs beyond.

3. On your return, by the same route, enjoy all those views you missed on your outward walk.

Otters

Practicals

Type of walk: An easy level walk followed by a short ascent to a fine viewpoint.

Distance:	6 miles/9.5km
Time:	3 hours
Map:	OS Explorer 353, Landranger 60

NB: *No dogs allowed.*

16

Port Wemyss and Portnahaven

Park in a lay-by near to the pier, grid ref 167519. To reach the twin villages, drive along the A847 until you reach Portnahaven's primary school, on your left. Turn left here and continue to the sea, where you turn right. A hundred metres along after crossing the burn, you reach the parking area.

Portnahaven and **Port Wemyss** stand at the end of the Rhinns peninsula, the two villages divided by the Rainich burn. Portnahaven was built in 1788 by Walter Campbell, grandfather of Walter Frederick Campbell. The latter began building Port Wemyss in 1833. He named it after his father-in-law, the 8th Earl of Wemyss.

Portnahaven

1. Walk back from the parking area and cross the bridge over the burn to take, on the right, a pleasing new track. This descends gently to continue across shallow cliffs to arrive at the old pier and a small picnic area. Across the narrow channel lies the island of Orsay, with its towering white lighthouse. Close by the old pier are interesting information boards. Walk on and follow the

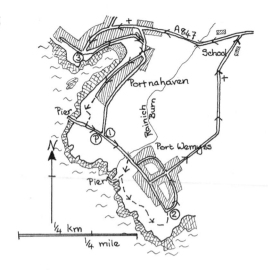

delightful track to arrive at the corner of the road, where it turns inland. From here there is a magnificent view across Loch Indaal to the Oa.

2. Follow the road to the primary school, where you turn left. This leads you over the dividing burn into Portnahaven. Descend by the 'main road' to the shore, and bear left to look up the stunning creek lined with picturesque cottages and houses. The latter stand on rock that in several places falls sheer to the water. Look for common seals hauled out on rocks and you might see a large grey seal swimming nearby. Shags sit on the rocks and sandpipers call from the shore.

Common seals

61

3. Walk, left, round the creek, passing in front of the cottages. No two are alike. Wind right round until you are near the shore once more. Go on to pass the more modern pier and on along a track to the road, where you continue to rejoin your car.

Heron

Practicals

Type of walk: Very short but the picturesque twin villages shouldn't be missed.

Distance: 1½ miles/2.5km
Time: 1 hour
Maps: OS Explorer 353, Landranger 60

17

Orsay Island off Portnahaven

Park as for walk 16. Ask in the shop or the pub for the name of someone who will take you across the little channel to the island (10 minutes), for a fee.

The lighthouse was built in 1824. It is in pristine condition, the brickwork white and the woodwork a soft ochre yellow. After landing at the jetty, walk the paths and wander the grassy pastures. Visit the medieval

Orsay Lighthouse and St. Columba's Chapel

Walk 17

63

chapel of St Columba: one gable end and four sturdy walls still stand. Stroll with care around the island; some gullies drop unexpectedly to a great depth. Notice the foghorn, neatly painted but now no longer in use. In the channel you should see both common and grey seals. On the island shags and most gulls breed. Look out to sea to see gannets hurrying by and cormorants flying up the channel. Before the lighthouse was automated the light keepers used to tell of the birds seen and how they remembered sweeping up barrow-loads of birds lured to their deaths by the light. Later, when a different beam was used there were far fewer fatalities.

Make sure you are waiting on the jetty for your prearranged departure time.

Gannets

Practicals

Type walk: Generally easy, but off the paths it is hard walking on the tussocky grass.

Distance: 1 miles/1.5km
Time: 1½ hours
Maps: OS Explorer 353, Landranger 60

18

Portnahaven, Frenchman's Rocks

Park tidily at the north-west corner of Portnahaven, near to the village's only pub, grid ref 165522.

Frenchman's Rocks lie offshore at the south-west corner of Islay and form a natural turning point for seabirds flying past. Especially if there is a south-west or westerly gale they will come through the channel between the rocks and the shore and give excellent views to the admiring birdwatchers. Here you might spot hundreds of guillemots and razorbills, flying south, low over the waves and quite close to the shore. You might also see gannets and, in summer and autumn, skuas especially great. Look also for storm petrels, kittiwakes and shearwaters.

Islay Shoreline Wave Energy Project (Limpet) is an experimental wave power station which sits astride a natural gully. The 'to and fro' movement of the sea water inside a chamber forces air back and forth through a turbine generator.

Frenchman's Rocks

Walk 18

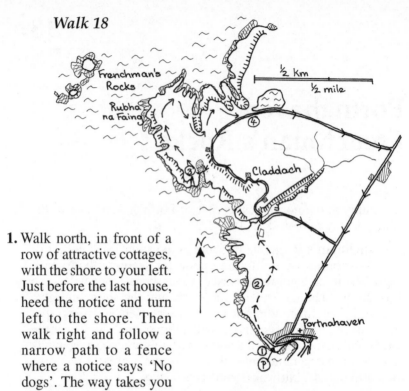

1. Walk north, in front of a row of attractive cottages, with the shore to your left. Just before the last house, heed the notice and turn left to the shore. Then walk right and follow a narrow path to a fence where a notice says 'No dogs'. The way takes you along the pleasing short-topped turf, between outcrops of gneiss. Here you might see many waxcap toadstools of all colours from bleached and creamy through to deep red. Look along the shoreline for a cave. Across the narrow channel lies MackKenzie Island, a neighbour to Orsay and its lighthouse.

2. Press on over a huge bay of large, wave-rounded boulders, picking the easiest way. Aim for a small gate in the fence, put there to aid walkers. Pass in front of the crofthouse and go on to the edge of a small inlet where turnstones feed. Follow this round right to join a narrow road. Stroll left, to cross a small bridge. Islay's experimental wave power station is away to your left. Climb the winding road to pass Claddach and walk along the high-level way to a small green gate just before the next house. Pass through and drop down the slope to a delightful sandy bay. Look for large clumps of sea holly. This increasingly rare plant has prickly leaves and pale blue flowers, tightly packed, rather like a thistle head. The leaves have a waxy blue coating that protects them from the effects of sea spray.

66

3. Look across to Frenchman's Rocks, lying offshore where you might like to pause and use your binoculars. Then press on ahead, taking care going round sheer-sided, deep gullies as you wind round the peninsula. Climb the stile over the fence by the second gully and head inland to join the narrow road once again, by a small loch.

4. After looking for red-throated divers and whooper swans, you might prefer to take the slightly shorter route back by turning right to walk the shore road to the T-junction, where you turn right to return to Portnahaven. For a longer walk, carry on beyond the lochan along the straight, virtually traffic-free lane to the T-junction. Turn right and stride another long straight minor road to return to the village.

Manx shearwaters

Practicals

Type of walk: This is a delightful ramble along the north-west shore from Portnahaven, which gives you opportunity to visit a glorious sandy bay, view the wave-station and bird watch the comings and going on Frenchman's Rocks.

Distance: 3½ miles/5.5km or 4½ miles/7.2km
Time: 2 hours or 3 hours plus time spent bird-watching
Maps: OS Explorer 353, Landranger 60

19

Kilchoman to Kilchiaran

Park at Kilchoman car park, grid ref 209636. To reach this drive the narrow road overlooking Loch Gorm, Islay's largest freshwater loch. Where the road turns sharp left towards Kilchoman, continue ahead down a pebbly track and on towards the sands.

Font, Kilchiaran Chapel

The partially restored church at **Kilchiaran** is possibly of fourteenth century origin. It is dedicated to Ciaran, one of the monks who accompanied St Columba. Go inside to see the font and several grave slabs that have been brought in from the graveyard.

After you return from Machir Bay you may wish to take the first right turn to go past the coastguard cottages. Continue down and then up hill to park tidily at **Kilchoman**.

Here stands the dilapidated, structurally unsafe, but still striking church. Near here the Lords of the Isles had their summer residence. Walk into the churchyard to see the fourteenth century cross, erected by John, the first Lord of the Isles. Look for the carvings of Christ, with Mary on his right, surrounded by saints and angels. The reverse side has intricate carving. The pedestal has four hollows, in one of which is an oval stone. Turning the latter was thought to help a woman give birth to a son. The churchyard has some fine medieval grave-slabs. Leave the church and walk back along the road to a stile beyond the second cottage. A path leads over the pasture to a walled cemetery. Here rows of identical

gravestones commemorate those members of the crew of HMS *Otranto* washed up on shore. The ship was lost off Islay on 6 October 1918, a month before Armistice was signed. Standing tall, above this moving sight, is a stone monument supporting a sword.

Kilchoman Cross

1. Go through the gate to walk along a track, with a fence to the right. Cross a small burn and continue, keeping between the sandy hillocks now on either side. Pass through the next gate and, where the track disappears, go ahead. Keep to the left of a small pool and press on ahead to cross a good track. Stroll on, keeping to the right of the hills now on your left, remaining parallel with the lovely shore. Pass several gullies in the steep-sided cliffs, bedded with sand. Soon the path becomes clearer (and muddier). Then pass a gate on your right, which you should notice for your return.

2. Walk on to pass through the next gate over the track. Just beyond, a grassy trod leads up towards Dun Chroisprig (the fort of the

cross) which you might wish to visit. And then you come level with a huge cliff face on your left. Here, with some imagination, you might see the profile of an old woman in the rock formation, locally known as Granny's Nose. Follow the track as it winds left and then curves right, up against the huge cliff face, where fulmars and choughs breed. Head on up the good track, now known as the Old Woman's Pass, an old drove road.

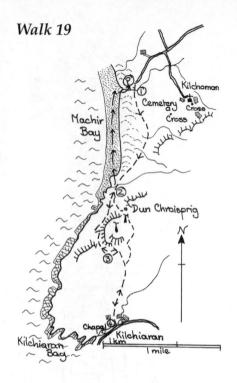

3. Descend steadily and follow the track as it winds right to pass through a gate. Go on gently descending, past MacLennan's cottages to reach the road. Turn right to visit the medieval church at Kilchiaran. From here you may wish to descend the track to Kilchiaran Bay, where there are some interesting geological formations. Then walk back up the road, past your return track on the left and stroll the few steps to Kilchiaran farm to see, from the road, the magnificent unique semicircular winnowing barn.

4. Walk back along the road and take the track for your

Hare

70

return, now on the right. Ascend to the gate and, beyond, stride the rising track to the brow. Then descend the zig-zagging track to pass below the Old Woman's Nose Crag. Carry on the delightful way to go through a gate and, just beyond, take the gate on your left, noted on your outward route.

5. Take either of the grassy trods that go on right. And then where they join descend, quite steeply, to the sands below. Walk the extensive sands of Machir Bay. As you continue along the shore look for choughs and gulls playing on the upwelling air currents. At the stream wind inland and wade the hurrying water. Pass through the gate to rejoin your car.

White-fronted geese

Practicals

Type of walk: A longish stroll during which you can enjoy the sands, the sea, a cliff-side path and an ancient site.

Distance: 5½ miles/9km
Time: 3 hours
Maps: OS Explorer 353, Landranger 60

20

Loch Gruinart RSPB Reserve

Park at the RSPB Loch Gruinart Reserve at the Visitor Centre at Aoradh farm, grid ref 275675. This is well signposted off the A847, Bridgend to Bruichladdich Road, and lies three miles from the turn off.

During the spring there are hundreds of **breeding waders**, lapwing, redshank, and snipe at the reserve and the nights resound with the call of the corncrake. Hen harriers nest on the moor and hunting golden eagles and peregrines occur all year round. In autumn thousands of barnacle and white-fronted geese return from Greenland and feed on the marsh, a sight not to be missed.

The **water levels** over the pastures and marsh are controlled by a series of sluices and ditches. In the breeding season, March to June, water is retained to allow waders to find food to feed their young. In summer, levels are lowered to provide suitable conditions for breeding corncrakes and to allow for farm work. In winter, water levels are raised again to provide feeding grounds for wildfowl.

Aoradh Farm Visitor Centre

1. Go inside the centre to see the many interesting and unusual displays. Then return to the road, cross and walk on along the minor road, running north. At a Y-junction of the road and a track, take the track and continue on down, following it as it winds right along a grassy ride enclosed within high banks. The banking is topped with gorse and on a sunny day attracts many butterflies. The high banks hide your approach from the many ducks on the pools. Go into the pleasing hide, where there are identification posters and books. On a spring day you might see swans, pintail ducks, godwits, teal, widgeon, dunlin and shelduck.

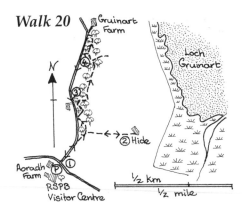

2. Don't forget to close your viewing window and then the door as you leave to return along the ride. Cross the track to go through the purpose-made gap in the fence opposite and climb up the reinforced way. Wind round right to reach the viewing platform and a seat from where there is a wonderful view. Continue on up the ride through gnarled willow and flags to come to a junction. The left turn takes you to the road, where you turn left again for the centre.

Dabchicks (little grebes)

3. To continue this walk through fine deciduous woodland, carry on the well arrowed and easy-to-walk path. The way winds through trees, heavily laden with lichen and moss. Before the leaves appear there is wonderful floral carpet of early spring flowers. Eventually the little path

73

comes to a fence, with pastures beyond where cows and calves graze. Wind left with the path, beside the fence now on your right, as it passes below seven-foot high bushes of gorse.

4. Follow the path as it joins a track where you turn left, then right again off it to pass below tall trees, mainly salt resistant sycamores. Here you might spot tree creepers. Look up to the tops of the trees to see a rookery, in early spring a noisy place. This is an unusual sight in Islay, an island with few trees to host these gregarious birds. On the trees, about half way up the trunks, are various shaped bat boxes. These house a male in each box, the females huddle together elsewhere! Walk on through the trees to join the minor road. Here turn left to return to the centre.

Ragged robin, water avens and spearwort

Practicals

Type of walk: Quite delightful

Distance: 1½ miles/2.5km
Time: 1 hour plus time spent in the bird hide
Maps: OS Explorer 353, Landranger 60

21

Ardnave Point and Kilnave Chapel

Park on grass at the north-east corner of Ardnave Loch, by a "car park" sign, taking care not to block vehicle access along the tracks), grid ref 286729. To reach this, leave Bridgend by the A847 and take the well signposted road in the direction of the RSPB Loch Gruinart Reserve. At the latter turn right for Ardnave, which lies three miles along a narrow road.

Ardnave Point lies at the tip of a large low-lying sandy promontory, which juts out into the Atlantic. On it grow some marram and much grassland, which provides grazing for a large number of sheep and cattle. It is partly sheltered by Nave Island and several smaller islands against which break gigantic rollers. To its east is the wide entrance to Loch Gruinart, where the tide races in. On the ebb, its extensive expanse of sand is revealed. Once the loch stretched further inland but the land has steadily built up at its head.

Visit the ruin of the twelfth century **Kilnave Chapel.** Look for the eighth century standing cross, still magnificent though parts of its arms are missing and much of its intricate carving is badly weathered. Go through the low entrance, which is arched with thin slabs of stone, and savour the peace within. Then wander round

Kilnave Cross

the older part of the graveyard, to look at the simple eighteenth and nineteenth century stone grave-slabs embedded into the turf. As you enjoy this delightful corner of the island, it is difficult to believe that in this chapel 30 men from Mull, followers of MacLean of Duart, were burnt to death. The followers of Islay's Sir James MacDonald exacted their terrible revenge because they believed that MacLean's army had murdered their chief.

1. From the parking area, look for the crannog towards the far side of the loch. Spend some time watching the varied bird life—you might see tufted duck, pintail or dabchick. Then follow the track round the loch in the direction of Ardnave House, a listed building with a crenellated barn beyond. Pass between the two buildings and bear left around a new shed to go through a gate. Stride along the made track as it moves out over rolling grassland. Ahead lies the Atlantic.

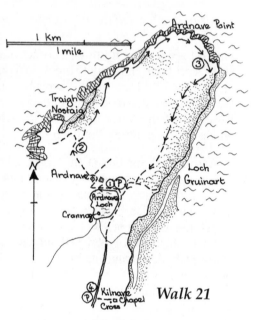

Walk 21

2. The track swings right to the sand dunes of Traigh Nostaig where it becomes a faint grassy track heading through the dunes parallel to the coast. Cross a wet gully where in late summer, the grass of parnassus grows with scabious, wild mint and ragged robin. Pass through a gateless gap in the fence and head towards the shoreline for a good view of Nave Island, with its ruined chapel. Close to the ruin is a chimney that was built when fish were cured here. Listen for the 'singing' of the seals as you go. Walk with care over the layers of grits and slates tilting towards the sea. Keep well inland away from the narrow deep ravines. Stroll on around the coast, where lady's bedstraw and small-flowered cranesbill prettily colour

76

the turf. Look on the shore for ringed plovers, purple sandpipers and oyster catchers. Look for otter tracks across the sand. Continue round the headland to look across the bay towards the hills of northern Islay.

3. Pass through the gap at the end of a boundary fence, close to the shore. Then begin to move inland, keeping above the enormous dune system along this eastern side of the promontory. Join a track heavily marked with tractor wheels and follow it through a gate. Look left to see the Paps of Jura, peeping over the northern hills Just before the track swings right, you can see the roof of a building on the shore. This was once a herring curing station. Continue along the track to return to Ardnave Loch. From here drive a mile along the road you used to approach the loch and park in a lay-by on the right. Opposite, take the gate to a track that leads to the ruin of the twelfth century Kilnave Chapel.

Purple sandpiper

Practicals

Type of walk: This is a lovely walk, culminating in a visit to a fine ruin.

Distance: 4 miles/6.5km
Time: 3 hours (including the visit to the ruined church)
Maps: OS Explorer 353, Landranger 60

22

Killinallan and Traigh Baile Aonghais

Park on the east side of Loch Gruinart at the gated end of the minor road that leads, after a mile, to Killinallan farm, grid ref 302708.

Sand dunes develop as a result of sand particles blown by the wind. The size and shape varies enormously according to the volume of sand, wind strength and direction. Some dunes reach a height of 30m whilst some low flat sandy plains occur a little above sea-level.

Waterfall, Gortantoid River

In many areas dunes form the first line of sea defence work and **marram grass** has been planted in many schemes. The common marram grass with wiry tufted leaves and whitish flower spikes is the main builder of sand dunes along our coasts. Its flinty leaves withstand rough winds and catch sand blown up from the beaches so that it collects in hummocks around them, all helping the sand hills to become stabilised.

Walk 22

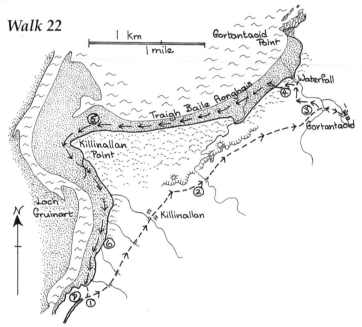

1. Walk on along the minor road to go through the pedestrian gate beside the padlocked farm gate. Here, on the gate, a notice gives you the phone number for the gamekeeper to check whether there is any deer shooting taking place (July 1 to October 20—but not on Sundays). A few yards along the good track, an upright slab of stone marked with a white arrow, directs walkers towards the shore for those who prefer to reverse the route of this walk if the tide is low. This walk description saves the shore walk for your return. Carry on to pass Killinallan farmhouse away to your left and its outbuildings to your right, with a fine range of hills to your far right. Stroll on along the fenced track through pastures, and where it becomes fenced on one side only. Ahead, Colonsay comes into view.

Sanderling

2. Soon the fencing ends and the track leads out into open pastures, with brief glimpses of one of the Paps on Jura overtopping the nearer Islay hills. Go on to pass an area of deep hollows, defended by spiky craggy outcrops, with a narrow burn hurrying to the shore, which is very close now. Just beyond this fascinating area, pass another arrow on a slab, directing you on an easy route to the shore.

3. Stroll on along the distinct track to come to a small quarry, just before a copse of alders about the Gortantaoid River. Between the quarry and the trees stands another arrowed slab. This one you do follow to take a clear path that eventually reaches a gate into the dunes. Before you pass through, walk over, right, to the side of the river to see a charming, tempestuous waterfall as the river hastens to the sea.

4. Go through the gate, walk right and follow the little path as it winds left. And then go through the first opening in the dunes to descend to the glorious sands of Traigh Baile Aonghais. Walk left to begin a leisurely return. Look for the many interesting shells on the beach. Look out to sea to watch the gannets dive and for the pretty little kittiwakes as they hurry above the waves. Look for sanderlings hunting for minute prey on the stranded seaweed and for a 'flurry' of ringed plovers chasing sand flies. Several shallow streams wander over the sands on their way to the sea and these you will need to wade or hop across.

5. Gradually the dunes, their sand held by marram grass, begin to tower higher and higher, until some are over 5m tall. As you go check the tide and also notice where you can escape through the dunes if you need to. Wind round the enormously high dunes at Killinallan Point, where a peep at the map will show you the density of the dune system here. Look out on the sand banks of the loch, if the tide is low, to see many seals hauled out and listen for their 'singing'.

6. Eventually you come to a small area of salt marsh. Beyond, wind round some rocky outcrops and a stretch of scattered rocks. Then weave between tussocks of grass and more rocks. Join a seaweedy track to a gate then aim towards the locked farm gate, passed at the start of the walk. Turn right, go through the small gate to return to your vehicle.

Snow Buntings

Practicals

Type of walk: This is a very satisfactory level walk with a good track taking you through pastures followed by a splendid return along the coast and the magnificent shore of Loch Gruinart.

Distance: 7½ miles/12km
Time: 3–4 hours
Map: OS Explorer 353, Landranger 60

23

Finlaggan

Park in the remnant of old road, grid ref 402677, on the north side of the A846, two miles from Port Askaig.

The MacDonald Lords of the Isles ruled much of the west coast of Scotland and the islands. They administered their vast kingdom from **Finlaggan,** which was the home of the chiefs from the twelfth to fifteenth century. Here they met as equals, the kings of England, Scotland and France.

Finlaggan

1. From the remnant of road, walk the narrow road towards Mulreesh. The way is lined with alder, rowan, willow and ash. In September the verges support large numbers of the delicate grass of Parnassus against a colourful background of knapweed, field scabious, ragged robin, yellow vetch and corn marigold. Continue on as the way swings right to pass through moorland. Where you turn left at the signed track for Finlaggan, the narrow road goes on to Mulreesh, an area where lead and some silver were mined.

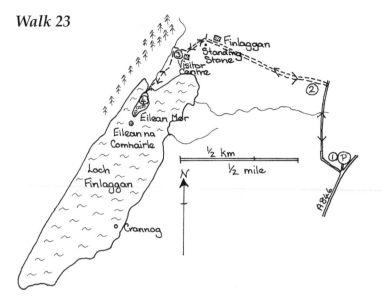

2. Stride towards the historic site, watching for Loch Finlaggan to come into view. It lies in a quiet hollow among the hills, where sheep graze. To the west of the loch, some of the heather moorland has been planted with conifers. On a dull day, when a slight mist fills the air, this site has a mysterious, magical aura. Go past Finlaggan House and look for the broad squat standing stone opposite. Turn left and walk to the well organised and interesting interpretative centre, housed in a restored cottage. It was opened in 1989.

3. Pass through the small gate on the right of the cottage and walk right to join a reinforced arrowed track. Cross several footbridges and then continue on along the fine walkway that passes through reeds and onto the main island Eilean Mor, the big island.

4. Here wander at will. Look for the gable ends of a hall and of a fourteenth century chapel built by John I, Lord of the Isles at that time, and dedicated to Findlugan, a sixth century monk who came to Scotland at the time of St Columba. Look for the beautifully carved grave slabs, once open to the elements but now protected. It is believed that the wives and children were interred here and the chieftains were buried on Iona. Access to the island at this time was by a stone causeway and when the water of the loch is low, traces of this can be seen. From the west end of the island, remnants of another causeway lead to Eilean na Comhairle, where the Lords are

believed to have held council, within a sturdy castle. This island and one further south are crannogs, man-made islands. The southern one is believed to have been used as a prison. In 1494 John II was forfeited by James IV. It appears that many of the buildings on the two islands were dismantled on the orders of the king determined to curb the powers of the MacDonalds once and for all. The reign of the Lords of the Isles was finally over.

5. Return by your outward route.

Grass of Parnassus

Practicals

Type of walk: Excellent walk on minor roads and a path to a lovely island.

Distance:	3 miles/5km
Time:	1–2 hours plus time spent in the interpretative centre and on the island. For times of opening of the centre, tel TIC 01496 810254
Maps:	OS Explorer 353, Landranger 60

Jura

Craighouse Bay and Paps

24

Inver, Jura

Park beyond the pier waiting room at Feolin, grid ref. 441694, where there are toilets.

Jura's west coast has some spectacular **raised beaches**. Low-lying parts of coasts are most likely to reveal these. Emergence occurs when the land that once bore the weight of massive ice-sheets rose with the removal of this great burden. The beach beyond Inver is about 31m above sea level and is composed of rounded quartzite pebbles. It supports only lichen. The lack of vegetation is due to the lack of soil as the quartzite is too hard to crumble. Look for an ancient wave formation over the whole, vast, magnificent area.

Jura has one long road, with very short branches going off to outlying villages. It runs for 32 miles from Feolin to Kinuachdrachd. It is mainly a narrow road, with passing places, the latter clearly marked with posts. The first mile has several blind bends as it runs between the cliffs and the shore and drivers should not try to enjoy the fantastic views. After a mile and a half, beyond

Raised Beach, Inver

Lealt Bridge (approximately 26 miles from Feolin), the metalled road ceases at what is known as The Road End. This is where the quarry parking is for the Glengarrisdale and Corryvreckan walks. Beyond, the road is privately maintained and vehicles are not allowed, but walkers are welcome to walk to the end.

To the north of Inver lie the ruins of the village of **Cnocbreac**. In about 1847, during the Highland Clearances, Cnocbrec was cleared by the landlord to make way for sheep. Some of the people emigrated to America and others moved to live elsewhere on Jura. The village is shown on a 1580s map.

1. Walk a short way along the 'Long Road' to visit the interesting and well arranged information centre at Feolin House. This is a fine old crofhouse well renovated and with extensions. Close by you might see deer strutting past to feed on the grass beside the Sound or in a walled field beside the road. Climb the track going off left, beside the centre, and carry on for 1½ miles. As you go enjoy the wonderful views across the Sound of Islay, where the Jura ferry plies back and forth. Look for gannets diving, kittiwakes flying up the choppy channel, and shearwaters too if it is very windy. You can see Dunlossit House overlooking the Sound and then the few houses at Port Askaig. As you continue the distillery at Caol Ila comes into view and then two lighthouses, Islay's and Jura's.

2. Follow the track as it descends quite steeply towards the shore. Look for the stone marking the grave of several sailors, on the right, as you near the foot of the slope. The victims were believed to have died of a fever while their ship was becalmed in nearby

Walk 24

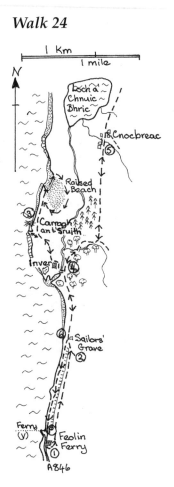

Whitefarland Bay. Carry on towards the white house at Inver, soon to pass through oak woodland. At the Y-junction turn left, cross the river on a footbridge and go on to pass through a gate on the right before the house. Here climb the track up through oaks to pass through a huge wooden gate with a sliding wooden catch. From now on you should see red deer. Follow the track and, where it ends, wind left, following a wheel marked track and keeping parallel with the deer fence, on the left, to come to the small lighthouse. This is the only one on Jura. It was built in 1960 and solar powered in 2002.

3. After a pause at this delightful spot, continue over the greensward, close to the shore and carry on to come to the vast magnificent raised beach. Walk across the foot of the beach where there is some vegetation behind the present-day sandy beach. Then wind right all the way round its edge, to rejoin your outward route. Return towards the deer fence to pick up the track taken earlier and descend to Inver.

4. Cross the river and, ignoring the track taken earlier i.e. your outward track on your right, wind left on a good track. Stroll on through more pleasing oak and birch woodland. Ignore the track,

Shags

left, for Inver Cottage and continue across a footbridge over a lively stream. Then emerge from the trees and follow the track through an open area, where you are likely to see more deer and also Highland cattle, all friendly but do not get between a mother and its calf. Follow the track past a plantation of conifers, on your left, and then out onto open moorland.

5. Go past the ruins of several crofthouses, Cnocbreac, close up to a barn belonging to the estate. Here in a lovely sheltered hollow you cross another burn on a footbridge. Then climb the slope ahead to see more of the ruined village. After a pause to enjoy the quietness and the view, return to the track and walk back to Inver. Just before the river, crossed earlier, turn left to take your outward track.

6. Pass the sailors' grave and then leave the track, right, to return along the good shoreline path, once the only way to Inver before the track on the cliffs was constructed. Again enjoy the superb view across the Sound and its bird life. There are three geological dykes that run down to the shore and the footpath takes you, easily, over behind these. Several burns come down to the shore, and if these are in spate, move down to the beach, so long as the tide is low enough, and walk on the pebbles. The water disappears through them. The path brings you to Feolin.

Practicals

Type of walk: This is a fascinating fairly level walk, with lots to see. Can be muddy after rain.

Distance:	8 miles/13km
Time:	3–4 hours
Maps:	OS Explorer 355, Landranger 61

25

Ardfin Pier

Park at the car park for Jura House, grid ref 488638. To reach this take the vehicle and passenger ferry from Port Askaig, on Islay, to Feolin on Jura. Turn right and drive the 'Long Road' for five miles to Ardfin.

From Ardfin pier you have a good view of **Claig Castle** on Fraoch Eilean (Heather Island) in the Sound of Islay. The island was first fortified by the mighty Somerled in the thirteenth century. It then passed to his descendants, Clan MacDonald, who for centuries were Lords of the Isles. It gave them control of the Sound of Islay, and they demanded tribute from all boats heading north. It is thought that the MacDonalds used the island as a prison. The castle ruins, seen on the top left-hand side, are divided from the remainder of the island by a deep natural trench (see map). It was abandoned in the sixteenth century. The island can only be reached by boat.

Pier,
opposite Claig Castle

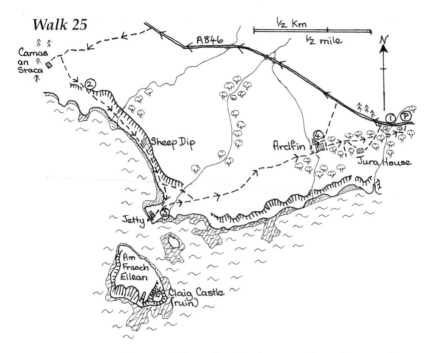

Walk 25

1. From the car park, turn right and walk the narrow road, generally quiet, for 1¼ miles, using the grassy verge for much of the way. When a plantation comes into view, take the wide track, bearing left, and giving access to a new dwelling. As you descend, gently, look right to see a 4m high standing stone on a mound. It is best accessed from the road. Carry on down the track until you reach a tall gate on the right, before the dwelling. Here leave the track, left, and walk over the rough pasture on a wandering green trod between bracken. Make your way to a gate onto the shore.

2. Beyond, go down a track and stroll on the distinct way, crossing several narrow streams hurrying towards the sea. Here look and listen for curlews. Go past a sheep dip, where the large pens are divided and enclosed by fine stone walls. Carry on along the track, winding round a delightful sandy bay to come to the tip of a little peninsula where there is a quay and a sturdy house. Pause here and enjoy the magnificent view and look across to Heather Island, which must have been a formidable prison.

3. Return along the south side of the peninsula and continue on either of two good tracks, with a narrower track coming in on the left and one going right, both of which you ignore. Climb the track going ahead and continue on past a small sycamore wood. As you approach Ardfin farm, follow the track as it winds sharp left and in a few steps pass through a gate, with solid gateposts, on the right.

4. Walk through the outbuildings. Pass to the right of the farmhouse, turn right onto a track and shortly, left to pass through a deer gate. At a junction walk left along a footpath, following a white arrow. Bear right at the car park direction sign and then left towards the road. Just before the cattle grid, before the road, turn right along a narrow path through woodland. At the junction of paths, turn right and then left to cross the footbridge. Stride left to go through a gate and then on to the gate to the road. Cross to the car park.

Curlew

C. M. Isherwood

Practicals

Type of walk: After the road walking is over, the track along the shore is a delight though wet in places. Excellent views.

Distance:	4 miles/6.5km
Time:	2 hours
Maps:	OS Explorer 355, Landranger 61

26

Jura House to the Misty Pool

Park in the car park for Jura House, grid ref 488638. For access see walk 25.

The **Campbells** controlled the island in the eighteenth century and they built Jura House. Today it is owned by the Riley-Smith family. A gate opposite the car park, the latter once the smithy for the house, gives access to the fine woodlands and gardens of the house. The Abhainn Bheag (the little river) once provided water for the village of Brosdale and the smithy.

Brosdale (broad dale) crofting township, which once stood just north of the cliff path, offended the laird's wife by spoiling her view from Jura House. In the 1840s she transported the community to a new village (New Brosdale) she had built for them above the 'Long Road' then completely demolished the old settlement. The villagers disliked their new homes, built in a hollow with no view, and the new houses were soon deserted.

Chambered Cairn, Poll a'Cheo

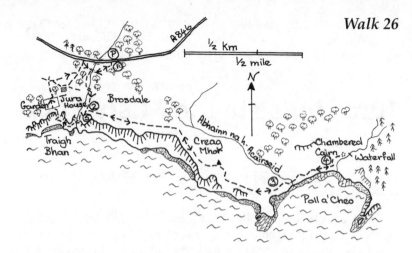

1. Cross the road from the car park to go through the gate. Follow the good path to pass through the next gate and go on over the burn by a sturdy bridge to a notice board with a welcome sign to Jura House. Here follow the signs for Walk B, waymarked with yellow arrows, and walk left down by the burn. Cross the next bridge and a ride and follow an arrow to walk beside the burn on your right. Just before the next bridge, turn left and go through a gate. Carry on down beside the fence on your right to reach the fenced cliffs very high above the shore from where you have a good view of MacArthur's Head lighthouse.

2. Ignore the kissing gate in the corner and walk left beside the fence on your right. Carry on the pleasing way, past a few traces of the ruins of Brosdale. Go through a gate and then follow the path as it winds right and climbs steeply and continues on a breezy way inside the fence. Where a line of fencing turns down to the shore, look for the villager's path. They carried seaweed up this path to fertilise their lazybeds for growing potatoes. Carry on along the cliffs, soon to follow the line of fencing as it descends towards the shore. The path passes first through bracken and then down through a gap in a wall and on out onto green sward above the shore. Pause on the way down, to enjoy a good view of Brosdale Island.

3. Carry on around the bay, Poll a' Cheo', to arrive at the stream Abhainn na h-Acairseid (the stream of anchorage). Here was the site of Portan Tigh-shalain, port of the salt house, where a year's supply was unloaded for the estate. No trace of the house remains.

94

Cross the burn just above its mouth, making use of grass-topped clumps before going over the generally shallow but slippery pebbly stream bed. Pick your way around the bay on an indistinct, winding path, walking between rocky outcrops, around little stretches of bog and sometimes on the sandy shore. Step across several small streams, where you might disturb a heron. Carry on the pleasing, challenging way until you reach the burn, Abhainn na Sroine at the far end of the bay.

4. Do not cross, but walk upstream. Wind round a clump of gorse on a boggy path to come to two small upright slabs of stone on a grassy hillock. These are portal stones of Jura's only neolithic chambered cairn, dating from around 2000 BC. Beyond the two uprights are several horizontal slabs. After a pause in this delightful sheltered corner, walk on up the little path to see a superb waterfall, plummeting into a swirling plunge pool, the 'misty pool'. Then make your return, using your outward route until you reach the stile in the corner, which you ignored much earlier. This time pass through.

5. Walk on ahead to a seat on the cliff edge, from where there is a fantastic view. Return along the path to join steps that wind round left and go down, steeply, beside a small stream, with a huge cliff face to your left. At the foot of steps, bear right to cross two footbridges and stroll across an area of rounded pebbles on the shore. Go through a gap in the wall and follow the path slightly inland. The way soon curves right and climbs more steps. Go through a gate, ignore the gate on the right and wind on up. Cross a footbridge and carry on.

Heron

95

Then take the gate on the right into the 'gardeners' shed' and out the other side. Choose a path to cross over the lovely walled gardens and leave by a green gate in an enormously high wall. Turn right and follow this track round left and up through sycamores. Go on the waymarked track, with Jura House to your right. Follow the sign for the car park. Just before the cattle grid, before the road, turn right onto a narrow path and then right again to cross the footbridge on your left. Bear left to return to the car park.

Snipe

Practicals

Type of walk: Full of contrasts. Cliff and challenging shore paths, a good waterfall, an ancient monument and delightful gardens in which to linger.

Distance: 4 miles/6.5km
Time: 2–3 hours
Maps: OS Explorer 355, Landranger 61

Market Loch, (Loch a'Bhaile-Mhargaidh)

Park in Craighouse, grid ref 528669.

Cattle from Islay were sent to markets at Crieff and Stirling on the mainland. They were made to swim the Sound of Islay to reach Feolin, then were walked over the hills to come down to Small Isles Bay near Keils or to descend to Lagg. Market Loch lies on one of the routes the cattle used. Today there is no trace, on this walk, of the old drove road.

1. Walk from Craighouse, along the 'Long Road' in the direction of Feolin for just over half a mile passing, on your right, the bonded warehouse for Jura distillery. Just before the signboard for Crackaig at the start of its access track, take the track opposite, leading towards the forest. Very soon you enter a large plantation of tall conifers. Follow the forest track as it bears left and then, when opposite the first turn on the right, pause. Here in a rough clearing, look left to see a tall standing stone, over 2m high. Beside it two others lie on the ground. These are known as the 'stones of the glen'.

2. Walk on along the continuing track and as you near the fence before the Allt Carragh a' Ghlinne, take a narrow

Stone of the Glen

97

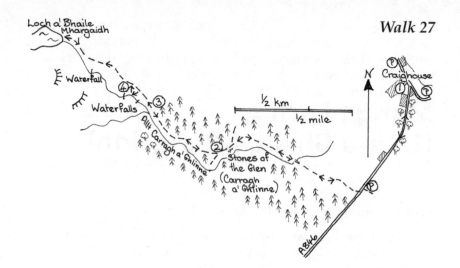

indistinct path into the trees on your right. Carry on up the pleasing way and also where the needle-strewn path moves out of the trees. Here you might see a tree creeper climbing a tree trunk, probing for insects in the crevices of the bark. Take care where the path, scored with tree roots, teeters on the edge of the deep, sheer drop to the tumbling burn far below. At one point, in high summer, you have to push through head high bracken. Pause to admire the spectacular waterfall on the burn as it plummets all the way down its gorge ahead, though much of its impetuosity is hidden by the lush vegetation of the magnificent glen. Eventually the path moves a little away from the edge and continues through the forest.

Wren

3. Where the plantation ends, climb steeply right to pass through a broken fence edging the gorge and continue, just as steeply, on a little path. Then the gradient eases and the path carries on across fairly level moorland, some distance from the burn. Follow a smaller path, left through heather, to the top of the gorge to see two more waterfalls, neither as big as the one lower down but both much more visible and quite superb after rain.

4. Return to the main path and begin climbing once more. The burn passes through a substantial wall but you should remain on the side you are on. Climb up a bank and wind round to the right of a small conical hill (the wall goes round the left side of it). Carry on up until you meet the wall and the clear path, which runs beside it. Do not be tempted to go through one of the gaps. Soon the loch comes into view, sparkling blue in a bowl in the low hills. After you have enjoyed this vista, return by your outward route.

Practicals

Type of walk: Fairly challenging for those with a good head for heights as you walk along the edge of parts of gorge. Children should be under tight control. The waterfalls are best seen after rain but remember that the path and the tree roots will be slippery. The climb to the loch is steep in parts but the reward of Market Loch in its hollow make it all worth the effort.

Distance: 4½ miles/7.4km
Time: 2–3 hours
Maps: OS Explorer 355, Landranger 61

28

Craighouse to Crackaig

Park in Craighouse, grid ref 528669.

Craighouse is the largest settlement on Jura. The 'long road' passes between the Jura Hotel and the distillery and then over Mill Burn. Beyond is the excellent village shop. The village has a pier, much in use when first built but since Caledonian MacBrayne ferries no longer call, the pier is now looking sad and neglected. It is used mainly by fishing boats and boats carrying a bulky cargo. Further along the road is the parish church and then the school.

Crackaig Bay

1. Walk in front of the hotel and cross the road bridge over the burn. Wind right uphill to pass the fire station and continue until you have gone by the first cottage, on the left. Immediately after, turn left to walk to a gate and, beyond, follow the path through a grassy clearing, where devil's-bit scabious and tormentil flower in early September, and is surrounded by trees. Go through a deer gate and carry on with birch woodland to the left and rough grassland to the right. Pause to look back to enjoy a fine view of Craighouse, with the magnificent Paps beyond. Follow the path into bracken and mixed woodland, cross a burn and then go on to a large clearing with woodland and hedgerows all around.

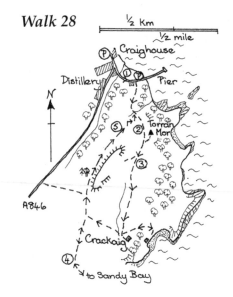

Walk 28

2. Leave the clearing by the top right corner and follow a wheel-marked track. Ascend a slope and, once on the brow, follow a narrow path going off left. Climb up through cushions of heather to the top of the small hill, Torran Mor, 75m, from where you have a breathtaking view of Small Isles Bay and across to mainland Scotland. This is a lovely hillock, where you will want to linger. Descend by the same route and follow the vehicle track on to pass through a deer gate, with a row of hillocks to your right and a low hillock to your left.

3. Where the vehicle track swings up right, leave it and walk ahead across the moor. Pass through a gap in a turf bank and head on towards Crackaig farmhouse; make for the left side of the shallow valley but after heavy rain you will have to pick your way carefully. On reaching the access track, turn left to walk a newly made track, before reaching the house. Follow it as it winds left and then descends, right, towards a rocky bay. Pass behind two holiday homes and then turn left to walk onto the shore where you will want to pause. Then return up the newly made track and carry on past the farmhouse and where it winds right to come to a gate across it. Here you might wish to make a diversion to delightful Sandy Bay, a great contrast to the rocky, pebbly bay just visited. If so, go through a gate on the left and strike across a pasture to go through another gate. Press on over the next pasture to another gate and then descend a path leading down to the lovely little bay.

4. Return from the bay by the outward route to rejoin the access track to Crackaig and this time pass through the gate mentioned earlier. Beyond, after a few steps, take a grassy track, right. Follow this as it passes an old caravan, on the left, and then wind round, right, on the lower slopes of a hillock on the right. Continue ahead to a few scattered trees and a bush on the skyline heading over rough pasture. Go on, still ahead, with a hedge line to your left to a few more straggly trees, and then go on down a bank to a ladderstile over a deer fence.

5. Beyond, walk ahead through rampant bushes and then go steadily left following a narrow winding path through more bushes to arrive at a better path, the one taken on your outward route, just before the second clearing. Turn left to pass through woodland and on through the first clearing to go through the deer gate. Walk on to arrive at the gate and then the road. Turn right and then wind left to reach the village.

Sneezewort and Devil's bit scabious

Practicals

Type of walk: A very pleasant afternoon's ramble.

Distance: 3 miles/5km
Time: 1–2 hours
Maps: OS Explorer 355, Landranger 61

NB *When the authors walked this way the return route was flagged with red and white plastic ties. These delineated the route that had been used for a race for the island's youngsters.*

29

Keils and Kilearnadail

Park in Craighouse, in the parking area beyond the Jura Hotel or at the pier, grid ref 528669.

Kilearnadail was the original site of Jura's parish church of which no trace now remains. Its cemetery sits in a tree-lined glen with hills beyond. It is a raised churchyard and has been, unusually, extended forward. Walk between the gravestones and several medieval grave-slabs to see the large, ornate Campbell mausoleum, erected in 1838. The area is now a protected site. Behind the cemetery are the ruins of two houses, where the family members all died of a disease and the houses were burnt.

Cottage, Keils

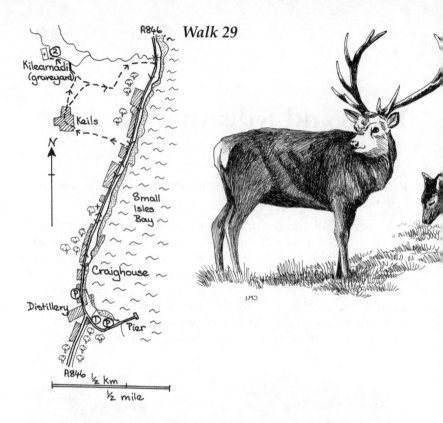

Walk 29

Kilearnadil
(graveyard)

A846

Keils

N

Small
Isles
Bay

Craighouse

Distillery

Pier

A846   ½ km
       ½ mile

1. Walk north from Craighouse along the shore road, where swans
   swim serenely and eider ducks keep in a companionable huddle,
   to come to the parish church. Here you might wish to go inside
   to see the lovely east window, which celebrates all the islanders
   who went to war and returned safely. In a room at the back of the
   hall is a delightful display of old photographs, starting from 1860,
   emotive pictures of times gone by: access is by an external staircase.
   After leaving the church and its hall, walk on for abut ½km to just
   beyond the post box. Here turn left along a signed track to walk a
   reinforced way to cross the burn. Follow the track round and pass
   through the few houses at Keils, a conservation area. Take the left
   track at a Y-junction, then at the T-junction wind left to come to a
   gate. Walk ahead to the cemetery in its idyllic setting.

2. After your visit leave by the gate in the wall beyond the mausoleum.
   Turn, right and continue below the cemetery beside a chuckling

104

Red deer

burn (Minister's Burn). Walk on along the path to the gate. Beyond go on ahead until you reach the shore road. Turn right for a leisurely stroll along the lovely coastline back to Craighouse.

Mute swans

Practicals

Type of walk: Short but very interesting. Some road walking.

Distance: 3 miles/5km
Time: 1–2 hours
Maps: OS Explorer 355, Landranger 61

30

Corran River and Sands

Park at grid ref 538709 in a large space on a track to the east of the road, 2½ miles north of Craighouse.

The **'Three Arched Bridge'**, as the bridge over the Corran River is commonly known, was built by Telford in about 1804 after a design by Wilson. Corran means a sickle and aptly describes the river as it pleasingly meanders on its way to cross the sands to the sea, neatly dividing the lovely Corran Sands in two.

Three-arched Bridge

1. Walk back to the road and turn right (north). Go past the old church, now a house, at Leargybreck and carry on as the road passes through a conifer plantation. In early evening or early morning you may be lucky enough to see a barn owl hunting in this area. When the conifers cease on the left, you have good views of open moorland, with Corra Bheinn behind. Then you reach the 3-arched bridge over the Corran River.

2. Do not cross but turn right just before it to walk a mown track, which runs between the river and the plantation. This is a delightful

3-arched Bridge

Corran River

Corran House

Leargybreck

Loch na Mile

½ km

½ mile

A846

way, with the river foaming to your left. At first it passes through birch and willow scrub where you may see great, blue and long-tailed tits and also reed buntings.

3. Cross a sturdy bridge over a tributary burn, then another. Ignore all the mown tracks going off to the right (there are at least six) and stay beside the river. There are benches at intervals where you can sit and admire the view. The path climbs a bluff where the river has cut a large bend and descends again beyond. It then winds round another big meander and then comes away from the

Primroses

river and a fence appears on the left. Curve round a boggy area and climb a small rise to be greeted by a grand view of Small Isles Bay and the splendid white Corran Sands.

4. Turn right on a lovely grassy path, which runs along behind the beach. Look for ringed plovers and oystercatchers here. Where the path turns right go with it to return to your car.

Ringed plovers and dunlin

Practicals

Type of walk: This a glorious walk, especially the path along beside the river and where it continues behind the sands.

Distance: 2 miles/3.4km
Time: 1 hour
Maps: OS Explorer 355, Landranger 61

31

Ardfernal and Lowlandman's Bay

Park in the parking area just beyond the Three Arched Bridge, grid ref 544721. This lies on the A846 3½ miles north of Craighouse.

Skervuile lighthouse, 1½ miles out in the Sound of Jura, is believed to be the first lighthouse to be built of brick instead of stone. Skervuile Light Houses, the shore station for the lighthouse, were built in 1861 to house the families of the lighthouse keepers. The cottage nearby was for the boatman who took the keepers out to the rock for their spell of duty. There was no road to the station and all supplies were brought by sea, with the boatman making regular trips to Craighouse. When the light became automated the shore station and boatman's cottage were sold and both became holiday cottages.

Ardfernal and The Paps

In 1841–6 there were 6 families, **36 people**, living at **Ardmenish.** In 1881 there were still 6 families and 28 people living there. Today only one house is occupied. For many years there was no road to the settlement and the postman walked across the moor three times a week. Today the postman goes daily, by van, along the track from Knockrome.

Walk 31

1. Cross the A-road, from the parking area, and walk up the lane signposted Ardfernal, with the Corran River hurrying to your right. Continue up the virtually traffic-free lane for a mile to pass the few houses at Knockrome. Go on up to the end of the road to Ardfernal, which now has one occupied house, two holiday cottages and several picturesque ruined crofthouses. Look for the kissing gate, a few steps, right, across a grassy area to start your climb up Ardfernal Hill. The narrow path is almost naturally stepped as it passes through heather to the cairn on the pleasing summit. The views are spectacular of the Paps and down over Lowlandman's Bay.

2. Leave the cairn and descend to go through the gate, walk over the little grassy slope to pass to the left of the three white cottages. This building was once four cottages and housed the paupers of the district. Go down the grassy way, pass a cottage on your left and go through a gate. From here walk diagonally, right, first descending a small hillock and then on along a raised way, once a track probably used by the Ardfernal children to get to school. Today it is boggy and often indistinct, but if you persevere you arrive at a gate across the good track from Knockrome.

3. Turn right, go through the gate and walk ahead along the easy way as it passes over moorland and through pastures. Ignore a track turning off right: this leads to the old Knockrome schoolhouse, now a dwelling, but once catering for children from all the settlements around. Carry on the gated way heading towards Ardmenish. Look right across the pastures to see the 'nick' in the 'skyline' of rocks that project into the bay to the right of the lighthouse station. A tale is told of the robber McLever; when trying to escape his pursuers, he leapt across the 'nick' and dived into the bay. He swam across to Arfernal and then swam across the next bay to hide in a cave in the forest. Alas he was caught by his pursuers while he slept, and was killed. Follow the track to the left of the outbuildings at Ardmenish and then, wind right, and carry on along it as it continues towards the peninsula that shelters Lowlandman's Bay.

Lapwing

4. Cross a ford and follow the often wet track as it winds right towards the solid lighthouse station. Climb up left behind the building and walk along the little ridge to McLever's 'nick' for spectacular views over Lowlandman's Bay and the little islands below Ardfernal Hill, where you might see seals hauled out. Return back along the track and just after the Light Houses continue ahead on a grassy trod that diverges from the track to reach the foot of a large jagged mass of epidorite. This is An Dunan, an iron-age fort, which is quite well preserved and well worth exploring.

5. Return to the track and walk on to cross the ford. A short way along turn left along a short track to go through a gate on the right. Step across a narrow pasture, where it can be boggy and ascend a grassy slope to reach a fine green field. If you are walking this way in the dusk you might spot a barn owl, eerily white in the failing light, quartering the grass for prey. Head up the field, keeping close to the bracken on your right, to reach a gate onto the track walked earlier. Turn left and carry on the gated way to the end of the track at Knockrome. Bear right through the settlement and descend the road to the parking area at the 3-arched bridge.

Hen harrier (female)

Practicals

Type of walk: An interesting walk through a quiet area which once was much more populated and busy. Generally easy walking, except for the rather wet area from Ardfernal to the main track. If too wet you might wish to descend to Knockrome and then turn right to walk all the way to Ardmenish on a track.

Distance: 9 miles/14.5km
Time: 4–5 hours
Maps: OS Explorer 355, Landranger 61

32

Corra Bheinn

Park in the first large passing place or lay-by, on the right side of the road, after crossing the three-arched bridge over the Corran river, grid ref 549732.

The Paps of Jura dominate the countryside around and can be seen on the skyline from the mainland and many surrounding islands. They are formed of quartzite which was rounded into a pap shape during the last ice-age. They have long slopes of scree thought to have been due to the shattering of the quartzite, by frost, also during the ice age. Beinn a' Chaolais (733m) has a long slide of scree, known as the slide of the old woman. The highest of the three is Beinn an Oir (785m) and the second highest is Beinn Shiantaidh (755m). Corra Bheinn (573m) is not a Pap. It lies just to the north east of Beinn Shiantaidh and is an easier climb than one of the Paps. The views from the summit cairn are superb. You can see Loch Tarbert, almost cutting the island in two. On a clear day you might spot Mull and the Garvellachs. Looking south you

Beinn Shiantaidh
from Corra Bheinn

can see Small Isles Bay and Craighouse, with Gigha and Kintyre to the south east. To the east look for Kilberry and Knapdale on mainland Argyll.

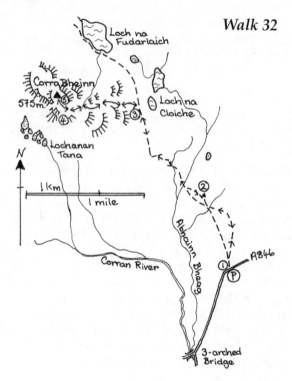

Walk 32

1. Cross the road from the lay-by and go over a rather slippery plank bridge across a ditch. Walk on along the good path to a notice board which welcomes people to Evans's Walk. The path was constructed by the late Mr Evans in the late nineteenth century to give him access, by pony, to Glen Batrick. The path is now rough and eroded in places, and boggy after heavy rain. Just beyond the signboard, the path forks. Here take the right branch, which is not part of the Evans's walk but is a drier way. Continue on towards the ridge and, just beyond, walk left along a clear path through long grass. Carry on until you join the Evans's walk, coming in on your left. Stroll on to come to a small stream and a large boggy area, where you take the right branch and head for a prominent cairn.

2. From here stride ahead to pass through a broken fence and then press on along the continuing track. At the burn, which you can normally cross on convenient stones, you may prefer to walk right on a narrow path upstream to wade across the shallows. Then return to the track and head on the cairned way. Cross a small stream and continue with the path as it bears right. Keep a look out here for deer, perhaps a group of stags or hinds, or a stag with his harem all about him, depending on the time of year.

3. When you reach a prominent cairn in the middle of a boggy area with Loch na Cloiche below to your right, look up left to see a perched boulder on the skyline. To its left is a small cairn. Here leave Evans's walk and head for the cairn up the almost pathless heather, tufted grass and quartzite, choosing the easiest route. When you reach the cairn look ahead to see a very fine cairn set on a large flat rock. Once you have reached this, carry on winding gently left and upwards over three transverse ridges. These can be ascended by weaving over grass and heather between 'plates' of quartzite.

4. As you near the left (west) end of the hill, the steepest but possibly the easiest part of the climb lies ahead. After ascending this you

Red deer hinds

suddenly reach a little valley just before the cairned summit of Corra Bhein. Once on top pause here to appreciate the fine view. Close beside you are the magnificent scree slopes of Beinn Shiantaidh and further on, almost hidden by the latter, is Beinn an Oir.

5. Then return by your upward route until you reach the Evans's walk, where you turn right. Follow your outward route, choosing the driest way.

Golden plover

Practicals

Type of walk: This is an exhilarating hill to climb, which seasoned walkers will enjoy. Remember to take waterproofs, wear boots, be able to read the map and use a compass. The walk gives you a real taste of Jura.

Distance: 5 miles/8km
Time: 3–4 hours
Maps: OS Explorer 355, Landranger 61

Glengarrisdale

Park north of Lealt, grid ref 671926, in the old quarry at the 'Road End'. This lies 27 miles from Feolin along Jura's only road. 'The Long Road'.

You are almost certain to spot a **hen harrier** while walking on Jura. Its usual haunts are moorlands, hillsides, marshes and open wastes. The male has a silvery-grey dress, almost black primaries and brilliant white on its belly. The female, larger than the male, is brown above with paler markings on the wings, the crown is streaked with dark brown. Most noticeable is the white patch above the tail. Both birds quarter the ground with easy flight, frequently interrupting their progress by hovering. They feed on mice, voles, young rabbits, rats, birds, frogs, lizards and insects.

Glengarrisdale Bay and Scarba

1. Walk on from the 'road end' for a mile, the surface of the track steadily deteriorating and barred to vehicles. Just before a chain

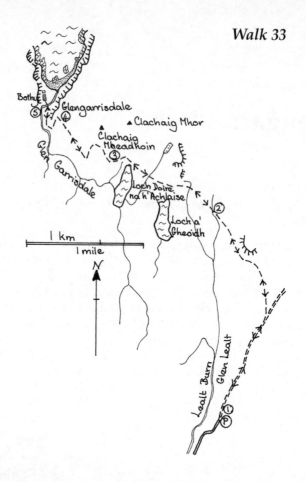

over the track, look for a delightful green knoll on the right side, much favoured by cows. The knoll lies just beyond a ladderstile over the deer fence also on the right. Here take the 'bridge' of stone slabs over the drainage ditch on your left. Then follow, over the open moorland, the tracks made by an all-terrain vehicle (ATV) used by deer stalkers. Follow the tracks as they veer right of an outcrop, on the left, and then continue half left across the moorland to step across a narrow burn. Walk on to come closer to an outcrop on the right. The way then descends quite gently to another easy-to-cross burn. Soon the ATV tracks spread across a widish area and disappear. Look on ahead to see them re-emerging from the mire and aim in that direction, choosing your own way.

2. Then you reach a wider burn, the headwaters of the Lealt Burn, where you need to find the best place to jump across. Next, climb uphill through bracken and then along a flattish area. Turn left around a knoll and away from the knolls, ridges and hills to the right. As you go keep a look out for a hen harrier. Carry on, climbing steadily and watch for your first sighting of Loch a'Gheoidh far below. From here on a clear day you might see the north end of Colonsay, with Mull beyond. Then descend down and down to wind right, still high above the loch and then on down to cross the end of the pretty Water Lily loch, Loch Doire na-h-Achlaise.

3. The ATV tracks then take you uphill again to pass below Clachaig Mheadhoin on a stony path, where you might come upon wild goats. Contour to go on through a col and turn left to descend quite steeply. Then the way goes left again and down a path through bracken, where you feel you are walking in the wrong direction. At the bottom of the slope, the tracks wind right on a good level drier way, into Glengarrisdale. Sadly this doesn't last for long and you cross a flat boggy area, where the tracks become rather vague.

4. When you spot them again they begin to wind sharply left before descending from this flat area to a pebbled path that takes you right and through a gap in a wall. Beyond, cross the dampish moorland, slightly left, to come to the Glengarrisdale River, which you cross on stepping stones to reach the Glengarrisdale Bothy on the edge of the bay. Here you will wish to spend some time on the lovely sandy shore and watch for otters and seals, turnstones, ringed plover and oystercatchers. Look right for a

Hen harrier (male)

Turnstone

stunning view of the rocky coast and a glimpse of the island of Scarba. If the river is in spate and the stepping stones well under water, make your way, right, across boggy patches and through bracken to come to a roofless ruined cottage. From here walk on along the side of the burn to reach the shore.

5. Return by the same route, always following the ATV tracks, which are a wonderful help in finding your way across this wild, glorious, pathless area.

Practicals

Type of walk: A challenging, exhilarating walk but, as with many paths on Jura, it can be really wet after a spell of heavy rain. Make full use of the ATV tracks that take you on the easiest route.

Distance: 8 miles/13km
Time: 4–5 hours
Maps: OS Explorer 355, Landranger 61

34

Corryvreckan

Park in the old quarry at the 'Road End', grid ref 671926. This is where the reasonable surface of the road ends and vehicles are not allowed beyond. Some people will wish to walk the six miles to Kinuachdrachd (and six miles back). Alternatively, you can take advantage of the taxi service offered, at the time of writing, by Mike Richardson, the owner of Kinuachdrachd. He uses a landrover. The track beyond the quarry parking area is maintained by the owners of Barnhill and Kinuachdrachd and filling the potholes, ruts etc is almost a full time job. The journey takes one hour to cover the six miles. This service needs to be booked in advance: contact by phone 07899 912116 or e-mail joanmikekd@hotmail.com. Accommodation is also available at Kinuachdrachd.

The **famous whirlpool** in the Gulf of Corryvreckan is best

Corryvreckan and Scarba

seen between flood and half flood and when there is a strong wind from the west or south-west. It lies between the northern tip of Jura and the island of Scarba. It is named after a Viking, named Breckan who wished to marry a princess of Jura. Her father, wary of this request but not daring to offend the Viking, suggested that the suitor should prove he was worthy of his daughter. He would allow the marriage if Breckan could survive three nights and three days in his longship anchored in the whirlpool. Breckan, advised by sages in Scandinavia, anchored his boat on the first night with a hemp rope and the second night, with a wool rope. Both broke but Breckan survived. The third night he used a rope made of the hair of virgins, unfortunately it too broke because, so the legend tells, one of the threads of hair came from a lady who was not what she said she was. Alas, Breckan did not survive the third night.

In 1945 **George Orwell** stayed at Kinuachdrachd and then moved 1½ miles south to Barnhill. Here he wrote the famous and much acclaimed *1984*.

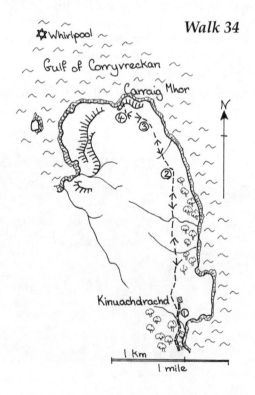

Walk 34

1. Just before Kinuachdrachd, which can offer accommodation as well as transport, a small sign on the left directs you along the old track, two miles long, to the Gulf of Corryvreckan. From the sign climb steadily uphill on a grassy path to pass through bracken to an iron gate. Walk on to go through a gap in a sturdy wall from where you have your first of many superb views of the Sound of Jura, with its islands, and of mainland Scotland, which seems such a short distance away. Walk on the distinct path, wet in places, to a kissing gate or take the ladderstile over the deer fence. Soon you have a fine view of the island of Scarba as you climb a small hill. Then descend, through an area which is regenerating naturally, to go through another kissing gate.

2. Continue on the lovely way, through carpets of heather, parallel with the fence, and then drop down the slope, left, to continue on a rising path that drifts right and contours round the next hill, with steep bracken slopes that run down to the shore. Pass very close to a lichen-clad tree and then carry on to step across a narrow burn. Go on to ascend the next hill on a good path. Pause here to look across the Sound to see the many masts of yachts at Craobh Haven, and beyond, Ben Cruachan, on mainland Argyll. Then look along the Argyll coast to see the end of the Crinan Canal, with the Big Bog (Moine Mhor), behind. Further right is the village of Crinan.

3. Carry on the distinct high level path as it winds left round hillocks to overlook the gulf. Look across the turbulent water towards the western tip of the bleak island, with its many high hill slopes. Then look a little right from this western tip to see a small bay. Just offshore (270m) is the site of the whirlpool. It is believed to

Sea eagle

123

be caused by a tall pillar of rock the top of which is about 27m below the surface. When the tide, driven by the strong westerly wind, hits the submerged pillar, water rushes over it, setting up the continuous whirling of the water. It is to this pillar that Breckan anchored his ropes.

4. Find a sheltered sunny spot on the high hillside to look down on the gulf. It takes some time to get your eye in and even though the whirlpool might not be at its best you will enjoy this lovely corner, where the very deep gulf is always changing at the whim of the tide and the wind. Watch for golden eagles, white-tailed fish eagles, buzzards, gannets and kittiwakes, the last of which, without binoculars, seem like tiny white blobs. Then begin your return by the same route to Kinuachdrachd.

Buzzard

C.M.Isherwood

Practicals

Type of walk: A splendid walk in this lovely corner of the island. Not to be missed.

Distance:	4 miles/6.5km plus 12miles/19km if walking both ways from the 'Road End'.
Time:	All day
Maps:	OS Explorer 355, Landranger 61

Colonsay

Kiloran Bay

35

Colonsay Pier

Park at the pier, grid ref 394941.

The **harbour at Scalasaig** is rather exposed and the pier, built in 1965, had to be strongly constructed with good fendering to withstand the pressure of the ferry in rough weather. At that time cars were lifted off. Later the pier was enlarged to take roll-on/roll-off ferries.

The **tall granite memorial** on a high mound, a good landmark for yachtsmen, was raised by the people of Colonsay in honour of the Lord of Colonsay in the late eighteenth and early nineteenth century.

Paps of Jura from Scalasaig

1. From the harbour, walk ahead to visit Colonsay's interesting heritage centre. Go on uphill, where in summer the road is lined with flags to visit, also on the left, the Presbyterian church, a plain building full of peace. Turn left into a wide track, beyond the church. Stride on, uphill, into the quiet moorland. Away to your right are two squat standing stones.

2. Leave the track and bear left along the ridge towards the memorial

126

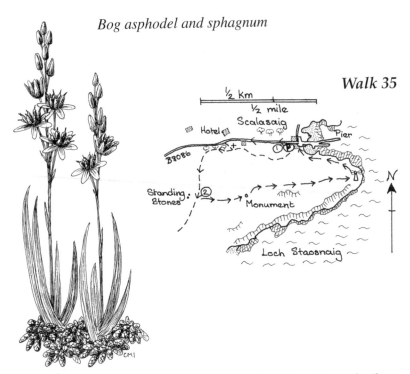

Bog asphodel and sphagnum

high on its mound. Pause here to enjoy the view. Go on in the same direction to descend the hill, heading towards the harbour lighthouse, gleaming white on the shoreline. As you go pass through, in late summer, aromatic bog myrtle and bog asphodel, so pick the driest way.

3. From the lighthouse, bear left, along the great whalebacks of rock, towards the harbour. Join the road, and turn right for the ferry.

Practicals

Type of walk: Short, pleasing walk. Could be wet underfoot when descending the rough pasture to the lighthouse, after rain.

Distance:	1½ miles/2.5km
Time:	1½ hours
Maps:	OS Explorer 354, Landranger 61

36

Beinn Eibhne

Park at the end of the A869, grid ref 373911. To reach this, drive ahead from the pier at Scalasaig and pass Colonsay Hotel on the right. After 1½ miles, turn left along the A-road and continue to the end.

A narrow footpath leads to the **monument to the McPhees,** very early proprietors of Colonsay. A plaque says that in 1023 Malcolm, last chief of the McPhee clan, was murdered by a renegade MacDonald. Close by the monument are the ruins of a chapel and a burial ground.

The Strand,
looking towards Oronsay

1. Walk back from the parking area to take a reinforced track on the right. This climbs steadily through dwarf willow, bog myrtle, heather, rush and hard fern. Twites sit on the wire fences and a heron wings slowly overhead. To the left lies Loch Cholla, which

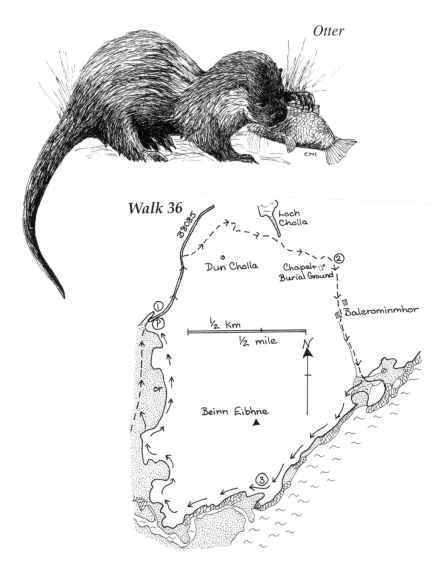

Otter

Walk 36

B8085

Loch Cholla

Dun Cholla

Chapel + Burial Ground

②

Balerominmhor

①
P

½ Km

½ mile

N

or

Beinn Eibhne ▲

③

CMI

supports a glorious array of white water lilies. Then the Paps of Jura come into view, followed by Islay. Take the narrow footpath, right, to visit the McPhee monument.

2. Return to the main path and walk on, right, to pass a house named Balerominmore. Stroll the continuing way, which is sometimes indistinct. Go through a gate in a wall to step out onto the shore.

Bear right. Here, the sward is a mass of low-growing thrift. As you continue yellow bedstraw mingles with the pink flowers of the thrift. Carry on along the dunes to pass two lovely sandy bays. Walk on round the low grassy cliffs, where basalt dykes stretch out to sea. Then as you walk, scuff your feet to hear the sands 'sing', as air trapped between the grains of sand is released, just as on Islay beyond the Carraig Fhada lighthouse.

3. Across the narrow channel on your left, lies the Isle of Oronsay. Contour around the slopes of Rubha Bagh nan Capull and Rubha Dubh, both overlooking The Strand, the mile-wide stretch of tidal sand between Oronsay and Colonsay (see walk 37). Overshadowing all is Beinn Eibhne (240ft/73m). If the tide is out, cut across the sands to rejoin your car.

Thrift

Practicals

Type of walk: A delightful walk. Some paths along the shore might be wet, but pick the driest way.

Distance: 3½ miles/5.5km
Time: 2 hours
Maps: OS Explorer 354, Landranger 61

Isle of Oronsay

Park as for walk 36.

Colonsay is an island of rocky outcrops of Torridon sandstone. The soil supports heather, bog myrtle and deer grass. Scattered over the island are cultivated areas where hay and silage are grown and cattle graze. The western coast is riven and wild with many delectable sheltered golden sandy bays. One great stretch, a mile

Cloisters, Priory, Oronsay

wide, at the southern end, known as The Strand, gives access to the delightful island of Oronsay. This small island can be reached, on foot, at low tide. Check the tide tables at the Colonsay Hotel or the post office at Scalasaig.

The Priory of St Columba, on Oronsay, was built in the thirteenth century on the site of a Celtic monastery. It is believed that the saint visited the island on his way from Ireland to Iona. Look for the magnificent cross and the small cloisters. Visit the restored Prior's House, where fine tombstones stand around the walls and two effigies lie in the centre.

Walk 37

1. Follow the vehicle tyre marks, generally those of the post van, across the sands. You should aim for the tarmacked road on Oronsay, seen before you start but soon hidden behind rocks as you progress. The 'track' across the sands first swings a little left from the end of the road where you have parked, then bears right before coming close to low cliffs on Oronsay by a marked post encircled with

Buzzard

yellow bands. The way then continues right, close to the cliffs. Here the track becomes a tarmacked road and there is a notice that says that all dogs must be on a lead.

2. Go on for a mile through quiet moorland and then the hay meadows of Oronsay farm. The road ends at the ruined priory. After you have explored the priory return by the same route. On the way you might spot a family of buzzards on the outcrops of Beinn Oronsay (230ft/70m).

Skylark

Practicals

Type of walk: Easy—but check the time of the tides and leave yourself time to visit the priory and return safely, without getting wet. The Strand can be crossed in walking boots or other footwear that you don't mind getting wet with sea water. You might get across almost dryshod. On a warm day it is fun to paddle.

Distance: 5 miles/8km
Time: 2½–3hours plus time spent at the priory
Maps: OS Explorer 354, Landranger 61

38

Colonsay's Rocky Spine

Park near the pier, grid ref 394941.

Colonsay House was built in 1722. Successive lairds have enlarged the house with additions in the style of the original building. Colonsay House gardens, with their magnificent display of rhododendrons, are open to the public.
Rocks, streams and contours around the house have been used to create a natural woodland garden. The shelter provided by the trees and the mildness of the climate allow many tender and rare shrubs from all parts of the world to flourish.

Drinking cup chained to a rock

1. Leave the pier at Scalasaig and walk ahead to the Colonsay Hotel. Just beyond the outbuildings, take the track, an old road, going off right. Pass the telephone exchange and spot, on the right, a standing stone set among smaller stones; the shape suggests a burial cairn. From here there is a good view inland across the island. Continue on where bog myrtle flourishes and heather covers outcrops of rock. Away to the left is Dun Eibhinn, once the stronghold of the McPhees, the medieval chiefs of Colonsay. Pass through a gate over the track and go on.

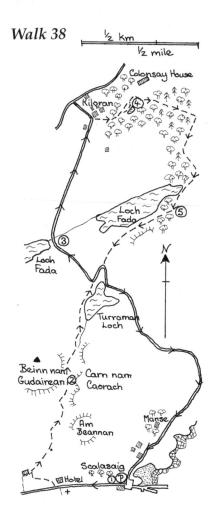

2. After a steady climb to the top of the pass, descend the lovely track, with Beinn nam Gudairean to your left and Carn nam Caorach to your right. Just as Turraman Loch comes into view, look for the well to your right. On the drinking cup chained to a rock the inscription reads, 'Wish your will, drink your fill'. After the lengthy climb over the hill, once the only route, a drink from the well must have been most welcome. Stroll on downhill, passing the dam of the loch, where honeysuckle clambers over sycamore and hazel. Emerge from the track onto a road, and turn left to pass a sheep dip on the right.

3. Saunter on between two of the three lochs, all called Fada, once one continuous stretch of water. Here in reed beds, listen for sedge warblers calling. Look left to the skyline above the westermost Loch Fada, where between two white houses stand two very tall standing stones. Stride on along the traffic-free road. Pass the village hall at Kiloran and beyond turn right to walk a reinforced track through the woodland of Colonsay House. Follow the arrowed sign for 'woodland and garden'. Go through the gate and take a narrow path, right, that leads to a pond set amid quiet woodland.

135

Then take another path, left, to return to the track again. Walk the pleasing way, where great bushes of rhododendrons support huge colourful blossoms. These shrubs grow among a large variety of tall forest trees, many from foreign lands.

4. Just before a holiday cottage called Avenue, leave the track, left, for another pleasant diversion. This takes you along a cleared way between more rhododendrons. On regaining the track, stride on. Beyond a buttressed wall on the left you have a glimpse of the delightful Colonsay House. Step out along the track and follow it as it moves out onto moorland on one side and woodland on the other. The shady way continues, lined by trees on both sides. Then, on the right, the northern end of the northernmost Loch Fada comes into view with large white waxen water-lilies on its still blue water.

5. Pass through the gateless gap and onto open moor, with stranded cliffs to the left and the loch below to your right. At the metalled road you have a choice, either to turn right to join the old road taken earlier, or turn left to return by the road to the pier. All of Colonsay's roads are a delight to walk and as you climb the hill (taking the second choice) you have a superb view of the Paps of Jura. Then Islay comes into view. After one-and-a-half miles, go past the old post office, to return to the pier.

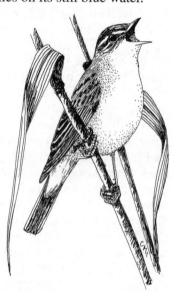

Sedge warbler

Practicals

Type of walk: A pleasing, generally easy ramble, with extensive views.

Distance:	5 miles/8km
Time:	3 hours
Maps:	OS Explorer 354, Landranger 61

39

Ardskenish

Park on the edge of the golf course, grid ref 361938. To reach
this leave Scalasaig by the A870 and travel west until you reach
the links below Beinn nan Caorach.

Colonsay is remote. It looks north across the sea for 15 miles
to Mull and south to Donegal. Westwards is the Atlantic and
eastwards lies Argyll hidden beyond Jura and Islay. But Colonsay
is not bleak and is very varied. It has wonderful cliffs, moorland,
lily-filled lochs, rhododendron woods, arable land, sandy beaches
and hills. Its annual rainfall is half that of Argyll. In summer its
hours of sunshine are comparable with those of Tiree, Scotland's
record holder.

An adult **corncrake** in summer is yellowish-buff in colour.
This is streaked and spotted with dark brown: the wings are a rich
chestnut. The cheeks and a stripe above the eye slate-grey and the
under parts, buffish with rufous bars on the flanks. It walks with

Ardskenish

its head rather low and its neck drawn in, lifting its feet high as it walks. It is a cautious bird and at the least sound peers with its neck stretched up for a better view before running for cover. When it gives its rasping call it points its bill upward. At the right time of the year it calls all night and if you are sleeping near a pasture where there are several nesting be prepared for a sleepless night—but what an experience!

1. From the parking area walk over the links towards the sands of Tobair Fhuair. Bear left and stroll around the bay, keeping close to the shoreline. Clamber, with care, up the great whalebacks of sandstone. Watch out for angry terns that dive at your head if you seem to be intruding on their territory. Continue over close-cropped turf, a wonderful flower garden in midsummer. Then begin to clamber up the clearly cairned Dun Gallain, where the sketchy remains of an ancient fort stand. Take care as you walk round the perimeter wall of stones as the cliffs drop sheer to the sea far below. What an impregnable look-out for those ancient defenders.

2. Go on round the cliffs, or cross the sand of Port Lobh (meaning Port Stink because of the decomposing seaweed). Stroll on across a large field of sea-rounded boulders tossed there during earlier storms and high tides. Again climb up the cliffs, keeping away from the extreme edges, which dramatically overhang the sea below. On the sward grows mountain everlasting. From this point you can see the isles of Tiree and Coll. Look landwards to see the

Walk 39

farmhouse of Machrins. Join a good track, turn right and follow this delightful way through huge rocky outcrops. As the track approaches sand dunes, look for a convenient sheltered ledge of rock to sit and sunbathe. Below, long fingers of black rock stretch out into the sea dividing the shore into small sandy bays. The track continues through a maze of sand dunes, covered with spiky marram. It ends at the farmhouse at Ardskenish. Across the dunes you can see Beinn Oronsay and, beyond, the Paps of Jura.

3. Return along the track, below the rocky outcrops, and then over moorland. Go on over the links, which are used as an emergency landing strip. Cross a stream by a plank and walk on to pass through a gate. Stride the good track. As you near your car, keep left (west) of the hill on top of which perches the coastguard lookout. And then join the road.

4. Stride on the quiet way to Lower Kilchattan, one of the island's three villages. Visit the graveyard, with its ruined chapel. Climb up the hill, passing the track to Seaview farm. Look over the next gate on the right to see the tall standing stones, glimpsed on the last walk. Visit the stones only if the hay has been cut, to avoid damage to the crop. Stand by the gate and listen for corn-crakes in the fields about the graveyard and the farm. Then walk back along the road, from where there are good views of Port Mor. Rejoin your car.

Common terns

Practicals

Type of walk: A good ramble along a dramatic coast.
Generally easy walking. Scrambling over the rocks is helped by their roughness.

Distance: 7 miles/11.2km
Time: 3–4 hours
Maps: OS Explorer 354, Landranger 61

40

Kiloran and Balnahard Bay

Park in the small area for cars at the end of the A870, grid ref 398976. To reach this, leave the pier at Scalascaig and turn right to drive the narrow A871 through the island, taking the A870, right, at the T-junction, to head towards the sands, where the road ends.

Kiloran Bay, a gloriously symmetrical curve of golden sand backed by grass-topped dunes, lies between Beinn an Sgoltaire and Carnan Eoin (360ft/143m). The latter is Colonsay's highest hill. In the bay a lavish ninth century Viking warrior burial was discovered. The man was laid to rest in his boat, together with his horse, weapons and ornaments.

Kiloran Bay

1. Drop down from the parking area to a kissing gate, which gives access to the dunes and sands. Continue north over the dunes, which are alive with skylarks and meadow pipits. Join a good

track also leading north. A steep climb takes you uphill, passing below Carnan Eoin. Then follow a high, flat part of the way before descending to cross one of Colonsay's many raised beaches.

2. Keep to the good track as it swings inland, first through heather moorland and then the pastures about Balnahard farmhouse. Just before the farmstead stands a circular building, pleasingly restored, where horses once turned millstones to grind the grain. Above the

Corncrake

farm and Beinn Bhreac you might spot a golden eagle soaring. Look for the standing stone to the left and then continue to the barn at the end of the reinforced track. Climb the stile and walk the path over the flower-covered machair until you reach a pleasing bay, a delight to swim in but colder than most on the island.

3. Before returning, you might like to walk to the northernmost tip of Colonsay. From the bay, head north delighting in the refreshing sea air and the lovely views as Mull comes into sight. Enjoy the peace and isolation before retracing your steps to rejoin your car.

Circling eagle

Practicals

Type of walk: An easy walk apart from the steep climb soon after joining the reinforced track.

Distance:	6 miles/10.5km
Time:	3 hours
Maps:	OS Explorer 354, Landranger 61
